A JAZZMAN'S TALE

A screenplay memoir of
1950s jazz trumpeter and pianist

Charles Freeman Lee

by Annette Johnson

A JAZZMAN'S TALE

ANNETTE JOHNSON

ISBN: 154464891X
ISBN 9781544648910

Johnson, Annette 1963 –

Printed in the United States of America

The photographs on the first and last two pages show the Wilberforce University Orchestra, *circa* 1890 on the front pages and *circa* 1900 on the back pages. All photographs in this book were provided under licence by the National Afro-American Museum and Cultural Center, Wilberforce, Ohio, United States of America. These photographs appear here on the printed page for the first time and are no longer available for licensing from the museum.
Visit www.ajazzmanstale.com and www.ohiohistory.org.

Charles Freeman Lee, *circa* 1947, at Wilberforce University where he played trumpet in Wilberforce Collegians. He was born in New York City on August 13, 1927 and died in Yellow Springs, Ohio, U.S.A., on June 15, 1997.

Time present and time past
Are both perhaps present in time future
And time future contained in time past.

T. S. Elliot, *Four Quartets*

Charles Freeman Lee, *circa* 1946, sitting atop his trumpet case as a member of Wilberforce Collegians.

Wilberforce University was the home of Wilberforce Collegians, a university band, with famous alumni - Ben Webster, Benny Carter, Frank Foster and others. In 1949, Freeman graduated from Wilberforce with a degree in Biology and left Ohio for New York City to play trumpet. There, he joined Monk, Elmo Hope, and Bud Powell and others in the revolution called bebop at Minton's Playhouse and the Paradise Club.

FOREWORD

When bebop came on the music scene, some jazz musicians embraced it with fervor; others ignored it patronizingly. Its improvisational calisthenics were too challenging for many of the established artists. But Freeman Lee, my one and only brother, latched onto it when he first heard it. The swing music he'd learned to play on his trumpet was quickly abandoned for bebop. He listened to every bop record he could find. He loved bebop.

Right after college, he hurried to New York, determined to become a professional musician and play bebop. He played well enough to get recognized as a 'comer' and soon he was hobnobbing with the then-new, now immortalized, jazz musicians, some of whom, like Monk, Sonny, and Mo, (Elmo Hope) he could call friends.

But Freeman had a problem: he could not seem to make a living from music. He also could not seem to distinguish between what was helpful and what was harmful to his career and his life. He chose bad companions, bad habits, and bad relationships. Ultimately, his career never flourished as his talent predicted. His recordings are only a small percentage of the ones he could have made.

His life as a musician took him eventually to Europe, where he found kindred spirits and gigged with other American musicians as well as Europeans and South Africans. This was a period of his life he looked on with great fondness. But on his last visit home to Ohio, cancer began its devastation of his body and spirit. He died finally in 1997, almost to the day predicted by his doctor — mainly I believe, because he was sick of being sick in Ohio. He might have been happier if he could have spent his last days in Paris or New York where, even though far from family, he would have felt that he was still hanging in there, being a bebop musician.

But those of us who loved him never calculated his failures. For Freeman had a sweet soul, a kind heart, a generous spirit. He would share whatever he had with whomever needed it. He was always there for me and always cared for me, his 'little sister'. He may not have been immortalized by the critics, but he is immortalized in the hearts of those who knew him well.

Professor Jane Lee Ball, 1998

The top photograph shows left to right: Mary Lee, Jane Lee and their brother, Freeman Lee, as students at Wilberforce University, circa 1946, while, at right is his sister, Jane Lee Ball, some 50 years later as Professor Jane Lee Ball, after her retirement from Wilberforce University, circa 2000.

"And most of the time, when you're young and dumb – you know everything!"
Charles Freeman Lee, bebop trumpeter and pianist, 1993.

In memory of all the jazzmen

CONTENTS

ACKNOWLEDGEMENTS

I offer my heartfelt thanks to Charles Freeman Lee, bebop trumpeter and pianist for his generosity and trust in agreeing to an Interview in 1993, on a cold European fall evening, in a café full of chatter. His patience, humour, and his insights proved valuable, as, I too, improvised my way through life.

I also thank Freeman's sister, the late Professor Emerita of English of Wilberforce University, Professor Jane Lee Ball, for her love, kindness, interest, support, gentle critique and dedication to seeing the project to completion. I also owe a debt of gratitude to Freeman's extended family - Janet Ball, Cris and Elizabeth Ball and Carole Ball – who contributed photographs for this book and offered love and support, as silent partners.

I am also thankful for the help and support of Ajola Burton, Alrica Henlon, Paulette Cowan, Michael and Hilory Pollard, Nadine Taylor, Dan Wright and Jason Baugh, who all made their unique contribution to the final product.

The errors and omissions are mine and for these I take full responsibility.

Annette Johnson, November 2017.

PROLOGUE

Charles Freeman Lee gave an interview about selected portions of his life as a jazzman, trumpeter and pianist in the USA and Europe. I got his story straight from him in 1993, in his own words, face to face, ear to voice, in a European café full of chatter, on a cold autumn evening. As a jazzman, improvisation was the main theme of his music. I discovered that improvisation was also the main theme of his life – not a bad idea, considering the mysteries, joys and heartbreaks that life often brings.

Freeman was a bopper, one of the beboppers, who took part in that revolution in jazz called bebop, that occurred in the years between 1945 and 1955. Freeman's interview was quite a ride and the verbatim excerpts in the screenplay show just how much fun he was, happy outlook, jazz lingo and all. The interview with his sister, Professor Jane Lee Ball, which follows the screenplay, was in a totally different key - he was talking to his little sister!

The screenplay is a story of love at first sight. It is funny in places and will make the most jaded laugh. At the same time, this screenplay is a love letter to jazz. I hope, you, the reader, will get that jazz feeling as you read. You may want to learn to improvise - get a *jazzitude*[2] to life – listen to your own drumbeat, solve your own issues, in your own way, by yourself and in your own time. Improvise, my friend - it's your life!

Let's make jazz fun again!™

---

2 A *jazzitude* is the wish to live one's own truth, improvising on one's formal learning from school, the media, pals and parents. It is a combination of jazz and attitude, a word coined by the writer to give a noun to jazz's relevance to life - when in doubt about the tune laid out before you, improvise!

A screenplay memoir of
1950s jazz trumpeter and pianist
Charles Freeman Lee

by Annette Johnson

INT. BAR, LE BAISER SALE, (THE SALTY KISS) RUE DES LOMBARDS, PARIS - NIGHT

Le Baiser Sale is a Paris jazz club, with a long wooden bar. A pewter bucket of Casablanca lilies stands on the corner of the bar. Black and white jazz performance photographs line the wall behind the bar.

The space is crowded, frenetic with pre-show orders. There is an anticipatory buzz from the crowd, below the LIVE HARMONICA.

A waiter, black vest and bowtie, weaves his way through standing room only, leans over, picks up a beer glass, adds it to the meter-high stack of glasses in the crook of his arm, which curves precariously to one side, but is expertly balanced.

He meanders through the crowd - *Excusez-moi!* - as people naturally shift to allow him to whizz through the swinging doors of the kitchen. The stack of glasses RATTLE, and the DIN OF THE KITCHEN SEEPS OUT as the doors open and close.

The ambiance is warm, earthy and Parisian – people of all ages, races and origins, from Africa to South America and islands in the Pacific and the tourists, Parisians for a day or two - gather to listen to live music.

WE HEAR APRIL IN PARIS

EXT. LE BAISER SALE, RUE DES LOMBARDS, PARIS - NIGHT

FREEMAN LEE, BILLY BROOKS and BENNY BAILEY are seated at a table outside the club. Wine, beer and cocktail glasses reflect the streetlights.

The trio look the quintessential jazzmen. Billy, however, is unusually diminutive and leans up into the table. They are in animated conversation, much laughter.

AS THE CAMERA APPROACHES, WE HEAR THE WHITE BLUES, SNIPPETS OF NEARBY FRENCH CONVERSATIONS, HEARTY LAUGHTER.

>   FREEMAN
>   Look up the definition of jazz in the dictionary. And look up the defini-
>   tion of music, and then improvisation, and see if it applies to it. They say
>   jazz is something to do with the rhythm of "negro" music! (laughs)

>   BILLY
>   (laughing)
>   To do with the rhythm of Negro music? Must be. Maybe the rhythm
>   was ours but the money they made certainly wasn't ours. I mean Louis
>   Armstrong, man oh man, he should have been rich, but uh…

BENNY
(nostalgic)
Yeah man, Freeman, I mean you remember them cats jamming with Big Nick at the Paradise? It seems pretty amazing now looking back. Those sessions were really swingin'! Idrees could cook, Stanley Turrentine was blowing everybody away, Art Farmer could cook…

FREEMAN
I mean, gentlemen, Dave Brubeck and Benny Goodman were supposed to have been king of something or the other! (laughs.) Yeah, Benny Goodman was an excellent clarinet player but, I mean, there were a lot of black cats that could play better than Benny Goodman?!

REACTION Benny and Billy - rhetorical laughter.

And Miles was a black cat, right? And everybody says, "Wow, Miles!" But Miles, as a trumpet player, he wasn't nothing special to us.

Bird gave him a gig, but if Bird hadn't given him a gig, who was going to hire Miles Davis?

I mean you had Kenny Dorham, you got Fats Navarro. You had a bunch of trumpet players that could play better than Miles.

And the thing about Miles' playing is that the he's easily copied. Chet Baker came right along and wow! He had Miles down pat! But, I mean you couldn't copy Dizzy and them cats. You couldn't copy Bird!

BILLY
(with bitterness)
And them cats never got where Miles was. Miles' sound appealed to the right people, so they promoted Miles and they got a lot of better cats… like, uh, present company not excluded! (laughs)

BENNY
I mean Miles could hold his own at the Paradise! When Big Nick call that tune - *The Song Is You* - he separated the men from the boys! All those changes to the bridge B flat to E to A flat to G flat - the cats who couldn't cut it would just sit it out!

FREEMAN
Yeah right. Miles was creative. And he was a good trumpet player! But there were so many trumpet players that could blow Miles away.

In his autobiography, he says, "Me and Dizzy and Clifford Brown…" I can't imagine him being with Dizzy and Clifford - not playing! I mean, yeah, hanging out maybe, but I mean - wow! (laughs heartily)

In 19 whenever it was that Miles started playing with Charley Parker, uh, there was so many players around that could… I don't know, man.

BENNY

And now the situation is like all these guys coming up now, most of them seem to be influenced by Miles or so it seems…

FREEMAN

Man, Miles was never an influence on me! I never thought he could play that good, I mean he could play but not a virtuoso?? If you're talking about creativity - he's original! That is one thing. He come out with one thing that was easy to, very simple, very easy to copy too, because copying Dizzy is pretty heavy-duty work!

BILLY

Yeah, Chet was definitely influenced by Miles, matter of fact… (wistfully) Strange, isn't. Then Chet went to Amsterdam and just passed away…

FREEMAN
(incredulous)
I know Chet Baker had Miles down pat, but I didn't realize he's supposed to have jumped out of a hotel window in Amsterdam, man. You've got to be kidding!

BILLY

That's right, man, he jumped, or he fell – nobody really knows. I just remember I was there, I had a gig at some place and I was hanging with Joe and next day someone called to say he died.

BENNY

As I recall it, Billy, I am the one that called you man – I was wanting to see him the next night.

BILLY

That's right – it <u>was</u> you that called. It's funny… yeah, I remember now. It was you that called to say Chet had passed away…

FREEMAN
(interrupting)
But Chet checked out early, I guess. But, I was a late starter with everything! (laughs) I guess I'll be checking out late...

The others join in the laughter and Benny orders another round of drinks from the handsome French waiter now leaning over to clear their table.

BEGIN CREDITS

NO SOUND

EXT. PARIS, L'ARC DE TRIOMPHE, CHAMPS ELYSEES - DAY

A lone cyclist makes her way towards *l'Arc de Triomphe*, head lowered in a determined stance against the headwind, as
the SWEET TONES OF A LONE STEEL DRUM ECHO, ever more clearly, bringing a gradual smile to her face.

She greets the STEEL DRUMMER at the entrance with a quick nod and rides under and out of the Arc to the *Place
Charles de Gaule*, towards a wide avenue (*Champs Elysees*).

PAN slowly from cyclist to larger view of *Place Charles de Gaule* and avenues radiating out in all directions.

WE HEAR L'ASCENSEUR POUR L'ECHAFAUD

VOICE OVER
It may only be coincidence that after four or five visits to Riker's Island, in
the tidal strait better known as the East River, Freeman found old friends
forty years later, on the right bank of the Seine, on the streets of Paris...

WE HEAR L'ASCENSEUR POUR L'ECHAFAUD

EXT. PARIS, CENTRE POMPIDOU AND ENVIRONS – NIGHT

Mime artists - including a clown - perform outside the Pompidou Centre as tourists and passers-by watch the
performance.

Crowds stream into jazz venues – Le Sunset/Sunside, Le Duc des Lombards, Jazz Club Etoile.

EXT. LE BAISER SALE - NIGHT

Freeman, Billy and Benny – now joined by many others at a table inside the club – are visible in outline through the
condensation on the window.

Talk is animated and dominated by laughter of the table-banging, doubling-over variety. The background crowd is sparse.

WE HEAR L'ASCENSEUR POUR L'ECHAFAUD

> VOICE OVER
> He was in the company of fellow trumpeters, Billy Brooks and Benny Bailey, both of whom lived in Europe, in silent exile from America. Purely by chance, perhaps, all three of them were born as the Sun streamed through Leo, passing over land *en route* to the Pacific, for if east was via west, there just had to be Indians in America…

EXT. PARIS - NIGHT

VARIOUS ANGLES OF the Eiffel Tower, the Louvre, the Montmartre district.

> VOICE OVER
> Less coincidental than this happy meeting of three friends, was the New Amsterdam Musical Association of New York, the forerunner of the Clef Club, formed by a cat called James Reece Europe at the turn of the century. For it bore a clear reference to the Treaty of Breda, signed over 300 years before, when the Dutch ceded New York to the British, more or less in exchange for Surinam…

EXT. PARIS, STREETS AND BOULEVARDS - NIGHT

INSERT series of road signs Versailles 20km Aeroport de Paris Orly 13 km.

Traffic, with beams on wet asphalt, moves slowly against the silhouette of the Paris skyline.

> VOICE OVER
> and bequeathing, among other things, the legacy of Harlem, or at least in name. This cat, Jim Europe, brought the Harlem Hellfighters, a pre-jazz ragtime band, to Paris during World War I. The Harlem Hellfighters toured 25 French towns and cities including Paris, France, and Paris, France loved them back!

EXT. PARIS, LATIN QUARTER - NIGHT

ANGLE ON a street-cleaning vehicle driving up a short narrow Paris street, the brushes on its underside rotate rapidly, leaving a trail free of rubbish behind.

WE HEAR L'ASCENSEUR POUR L'ECHAFAUD

EXT. PARIS, VICINITY PONT DES ARTS (LOVE PADLOCK BRIDGE) - NIGHT

The streets are a sea of young lovers kissing and embracing, giggling, laughing or looking into each other's eyes before locking their padlock in place on the bridge, which is plastered in padlocks.

Some lovers take pictures with cameras.

WE HEAR L'ASCENSEUR POUR L'ECHAFAUD

PAN to Pont des Arts completely covered in padlocks, symbols of young love fixed in place 'forever'.

> VOICE OVER
> In the New York of the bebop era, the deceitful ease of heroin was enjoyed by many. The tales told by musicians of brutal arrests and definite jail sentences for luckless users, should one fail to make a venal arrangement with the police…

EXT. PARIS, VICINITY GARE DU NORD - NIGHT

A gathering of heroin addicts, gaunt faced and hungry, focus on the fix, stooping, barely balancing on their heels, in their circle of desperation.

As they do their thing, four *gendarmes* come around the corner, and lighters, foil papers, spoons, straws and other paraphernalia fly into the air, as the junkies summon unseen strength and scatter in all directions.

WE HEAR L'ASCENSEUR POUR L'ECHAFAUD

> VOICE OVER
> might prove intimidating to the Parisian junkies of the moment, who so happily take refuge outside the Gare du Nord, huddled together, all the better to avoid the cops - *les flics* - the shivers and the man they owe.

EXT. LE BAISER SALE, PARIS - NIGHT

We see the silhouette of the trio - Freeman, Benny Bailey and Billy Brooks - joined by others, all of whom are laughing as Freeman holds court. Empty glasses of all shapes and sizes testify to an evening's hearty drinking.

WE HEAR STRAIGHT NO CHASER.

> VOICE OVER
> But then, all those bebop days were over sixty years ago.

FADE

EXT. NEW YORK BUS STATION - NIGHT - 1950

A bus pulls into the station. Relatives and friends watch its circular approach from the bay.

As the bus comes to a halt, the destination display-sign flips to Dayton, Ohio.

Freeman disembarks as the fifth passenger in line. A sharper dresser, he walks confidently to the bay, with no expectation of greeting a familiar face. He avoids the embraces of newly-arrived relatives and long-waiting greeters.

He heads to the waiting room.

Freeman places his leather case on a bench, begins to speak to its lone occupant, then thinking better of requesting a stranger to watch his case, he hesitates, picks it up and seeing a telephone on the floor above, he lumbers up the stairs.

INT. A NEW YORK BUS STATION, A PHONE BOOTH – NIGHT

> FREEMAN
> (with 1950's receiver to his ear)
> DACOSTA, what's happenin' man? Yeah, was kinda late, we just cruised in. (Listens.) Wait here man? You've got to be kidding. It's getting kinda chilly. (listens.) But, man… okay – I'll see you here in a little while, but it's really getting chilly so don't make me freeze, man.

EXT. NEW YORK CITY STREET - NIGHT

Freeman wanders around, hunched over to reduce the full impact of a light drizzle.

His eyes are assaulted by the visual impact of opulence – cars, sedans, cabs, limousines fashionably attired citizens and neon lights.

The sound of CAR HORNS is softened by the SWISH of wet traffic. He looks up at the gigantesque architectural structures and is impressed despite himself.

A shiver moves through his body, both in awe and against the cold.

WE HEAR MUSIC.

INT. BUS STATION, WAITING ROOM - NIGHT

Freeman is seated among passengers. His nerves and furtive glances belie the self-assured exterior.

He rises, looks at himself in the glass door, adjusts his collar and turns around to see Dacosta sauntering over.

                              DACOSTA
            (with a show of enthusiasm of one who owns the city)
                  Freeman, what's happening my man?

They embrace warmly, DaCosta's arm lingers protectively as he 'leads' Freeman to the exit.

                              DACOSTA
                  Let's drink to your arrival in New York.

                              FREEMAN
                  Man, you want me to get <u>drunk</u> on arrival?

Both men laugh and DaCosta's lingering arm drops.

INT. BAR/RESTAURANT SNOOKIES - NIGHT

The bar is crowded, and the patrons are mostly black. WE HEAR GOD BLESS THE CHILD.

DaCosta and Freeman stand at the bar. The BARTENDER signals imminent service with his index finger, as he pours drinks.

A waitress emerges from the door behind the bar with a tray of Southern delights – fried chicken, cornbread, vegetables of all colours - which Freeman's eyes follow to the table of a well-dressed obviously courting couple.

The waitress turns around and smiles flirtatiously with Freeman as she places the empty tray on the bar.

                              DACOSTA
                          (with authority)
                  Two double bourbons please. Neat. No ice.

He turns to Freeman.

                          DACOSTA(CONT'D)
                  Yeah, man, they've got a whole bunch of clubs uptown where it's real-
                  ly happenin'! You got the Paradise, the Bamville. Of course, the cool-
                  est uptown is Minton's Playhouse and a little way up from there is the
                  Nest. Everybody's up there at Minton's, jammin' every night of the week!
                  Midtown is cool too man, they got a place called Birdland, man, Birdland
                  – can you dig that shit?

Freeman listens intently but feigns disinterest as he sips his drink.

FREEMAN

So, this is your city, man, right? You're gonna show me some, uh, courtesy, right? Like a nice warm meal before you kinda give me, I dunno, man, the keys to the city or something?! (laughs). Then you can show me the way to WESTBROOK's. (laughs)

DACOSTA

(realizing his exuberance will cost)
Okay, man, let's eat, er, miss, excuse me, miss…

They swallow their drinks, glasses upwards, rise in unison and Freeman takes command of the situation.

FREEMAN

(leaning out into path of approaching waitress)
Uh, excuse me, my friend and I would like to enjoy a meal -could you show us a table? Please.

WAITRESS

(smiling warmly into Freeman's eyes)
Certainly, gentlemen! Come with me.

Freeman winks at DaCosta who smiles knowingly – the situation was equal, country bumpkin has charm!

FADE

INT. A NEW YORK CITY SUBWAY STATION, PLATFORM TRAIN - NIGHT

The platform is virtually empty and Freeman and DaCosta's RUNNING FOOTSTEPS echo in the cavernous underground tunnel before a train SCREECHES into view.

DACOSTA

(running)
Just run and jump with me!

The two men jump the turnstile one after the other, and just about board the train before its doors close.
EXT. HARLEM, APARTMENT BUILDING - NIGHT

DaCosta and Freeman walk up to the stoop. WE HEAR THEM SCATTING 'NICE WORK IF YOU CAN GET IT.'

The newcomer/resident tension has dissolved under the influence of alcohol. Freeman's arm is on DaCosta's shoulder.

Freeman rings the bell. A window SQUEAKS open four floors up, WESTBROOK looks out.

WESTBROOK
(with booming laughter and mock seriousness)
Who in the hell is down there at this time of night? You cats dare to come rappin' at this time of night? What in the hell?

INT. HARLEM APARTMENT BUILDING LOBBY - NIGHT

At the foot of the staircase with an ornate banister, Freeman and Dacosta SCAT TOGETHER and ascend the stairs. Midway, Freeman leans over the edge into the darkness and out of view. He stops scatting.

FREEMAN
(leaning precariously over the banister)
Why don't I just go over the edge, man, over the edge of sobriety? (laughs) Into the unknown forgotten darkness? Why don't I just blow my soon to be illustrious career?

DACOSTA
(restraining FREEMAN from his attempted jump)
Don't fuck around man!

Freeman encourages shared laughter.

INT. HALLWAY OF WESTBROOK'S BUILDING - NIGHT

The door swings open and we see Westbrook, a full faced man with tender unwavering eyes and a frank expression. His movement evokes simple conviction and unforced authority.

WESTBROOK
(ironic)
Step into my palace, gentlemen. Welcome to the Taj Mahal! (Booming laughter.)

INT. WESTBROOK'S PAD - NIGHT

DaCosta and Freeman enter, the greetings are warm but neither embrace Westbrook and instead shake his outstretched hand.

They glance around at the order etched into every crevice of the pad.

WESTBROOK
You cats want a beer? Though from the looks of you two, you don't need no more.

Westbrook gives each a beer and glass which he takes from the icebox by the wooden space-maker.

>   WESTBROOK
>   So, DaCosta, you're from New York City?

>   DACOSTA
>   (embarrassed)
>   No, man, I'm from Ohio, but I have been living here now for ages. Man,
>   I am a native New Yorker now.

>   FREEMAN
>   Yeah, man, he's so native he can go eat at his aunt's house every Sunday!

They laugh heartily. Westbrook looks at his watch.

>   WESTBROOK
>   Uh, you know I could dig it if you guys wanna hang and chill. I've really
>   got to shut my eyes this minute – eearrlee start tomorrow.

>   DACOSTA
>   (rising)
>   Oh, shit, it's late man, I'll see you around, Freeman. I gotta split.

INT. ALCOVE OF WESTBROOK'S PAD - NIGHT

Freeman is lying in bed in the dark.

WE HEAR WESTBROOK'S SNORE in the background.

The curtain over the rectangular window is blown up lightly, like the wind under a woman's skirt. WE HEAR ECHOING OF CITY DIN (TRAFFIC, ALLEY CATS), distorted through the small space between open window and ornate still.

Freeman suddenly sits up and looks in the rectangular mirror leaning on an adjacent wall and smiles.

>   FREEMAN
>   (whispering)
>   Man, I am in New York. I've got my friends and I'm gonna be okay. Just
>   cool, okay. Just cool.

Freeman smiles.

INT. WESTBROOK'S PAD - DAY

WE HEAR NICE WORK IF YOU CAN GET IT.

Freeman does the last of his morning ablutions – shaving in his t-shirt and pants. He then splashes on aftershave.

He whistles as he buttons his shirt, tops it with a blazer. He adjusts the outfit with theatrical vanity. Satisfied, he steps back and looks approvingly.

His self-admiration is suddenly interrupted by a bright reflection in the mirror – the sparkling coins in a ceramic dish on a table.

He spins around and walks over to the table, picks out dimes and nickels, turns and catches himself in the mirror. His guilt vanishes in a silent pledge to himself in the mirror "I'll pay it back." He pockets the change and departs.

ANGLE ON creeping disorder of Freeman factor in the otherwise orderly domestic scenario of Westbrook.

FADE

EXT. BAR/NIGHTCLUB THE ROYAL ROOST NEON SIGN - NIGHT

Ladies of the evening discreetly ply their trade under the Royal Roost neon sign. A few males deal discreetly on the far corner.

A couple exit the swinging doors, followed by Freeman who steps aside to avoid bumping into an incoming patron whom he recognizes as GEORGE RUSSELL.

George smiles, flashing brilliant white teeth, a fitting touch to an altogether handsome face.

> GEORGE
> Hey, man, Freeman! Someone told me you were in town. (laughs)
> It's been a long time since the tenth grade! And the Wilberforce Collegians!

> FREEMAN
> Yeah, a very long time. How're you doin', George?

INT. THE ROYAL ROOST - NIGHT

A female vocalist sings accompanied by a pianist. The patrons are mostly black, with a smattering of whites, mostly females.

George and Freeman empty their glasses, bang them on the bar. They weave their way through the patrons to the exit.

GEORGE
(looking round to address Freeman, who is following)
So, man, maybe I've got something for you. You meet me at Novostudio at 43rd and 6th on Monday, 11 O'clock…

FREEMAN
Man, I just got here! Give me a subway station man.

GEORGE
Take the A train (laughs at his own joke) to Lexington and I'll see you outside.

INT. WESTBROOK'S PAD - DAY

ANGLE ON Freeman's belongings sprawling and spawning all over Westbrook's domestic order.

Freeman exercises his fingers while doing his morning ablutions.

WE HEAR STOMPIN' AT THE SAVOY. HE WHISTLES.

Satisfied with his appearance in the clean circle he has drawn at face height on the otherwise dusty mirror, he steps over garments on the floor in rhythm.

Freeman then helps himself to change from the ceramic dish, spins around and takes his coat from the rack by the door. With a stylish gesture, he departs.

EXT. NEW YORK CITY SUBWAY STATION - DAY

George, dapper in dress, looks around and at his watch. He spots Freeman and whistles with his index finger and thumb. He skilfully crosses the street mid-traffic to the other side.

The two hastily shake hands, and George takes off with Freeman immediately behind. His pace is brisk and Freeman makes an effort to keep up.

GEORGE
Business is terrible, real bad I tell you. Things are bad. Not much work around, you can't be pickin' and choosing between gigs.

George turns the corner sharply at the end of the block, while Freeman straggles behind.

GEORGE
The worst thing they ever did was to get rid of Prohibition. New York City has been a bitch ever since.

FREEMAN
(non-committal)

Oh really?

GEORGE

Yeah. Well… a lotta cats say it – you know, secret clubs, secret booze, secret gigs – all that's over with!

EXT. THEATRE BUILDING, NOVOSTUDIO, BACK ENTRANCE
- DAY

The pair approaches, Freeman is still a pace or two behind. George suddenly leaves the pavement for a staircase and Freeman follows, not expecting the sudden shift.

The pair descended a winding, spiral metal staircase.

INT. HAZILY LIT LABYRINTHINE BACKSTAGE ENTRANCE OF NOVOSTUDIO - DAY

The pair walk down the main corridor. WE HEAR MISTERIOSO, THE PAIR'S FOOTSTEPS in heavy leather shoes.

ANGLE on the men's knees to floor, back to full body.

The pair turn the corner. WE HEAR the CACOPHONY OF A BANDWARMING UP in contrast to MISTERIOSO and FOOTSTEPS.

The lighting is half-mist. As they near the end of the main corridor, WE HEAR THE BAND WARMING UP more clearly.

As he makes his last pace to the end of the corridor, George turns sharply to the left, Freeman follows, looking expectantly for a band.

ANGLE on the men walking instead towards a large open empty space.

George, now a few paces ahead, turns sharply to the back of the room and Freeman follows. He suddenly comes to a halt looking straight ahead in George's direction.

INT. BACKSTAGE BAND REHEARSAL WELL OF NOVOSTUDIO - DAY

MISTERIOSO is cut. WARM UP EXERCISES cease. George's FOOTSTOPS are solitary. The subject of Freeman's awe, a band of two dozen or so snow-white musicians take a break from pre-rehearsal warm-up.

The BANDLEADER approaches George, who looks around expecting Freeman to be right behind him. He disguises his irritation at Freeman's awestruck stance and greets the Bandleader.

ANGLE on snow-white musicians and their instruments. All have now fallen silent. Some faces are sheepish, others show hostility, some are sanguine, some indifferently attend to their instruments.

Freeman walks right by the band, sits on the stage, places his trumpet case beside his leg. He looks at George and the Bandleader, who seem to be agreeing to disagree.

INT. HAZILY LIT LABYRINTHINE BACKSTAGE ENTRANCE OF NOVOSTUDIO - DAY

George and Freeman retrace their steps through the corridor. WE HEAR FOOTSTEPS, no longer in unison, and CECIL TAYLOR on piano. Freeman no longer tries to keep up with George.

EXT. NOVOSTUDIO BUILDING, BACK ENTRANCE - DAY

The sun streams through clouds as George and Freeman emerge from stairs. George offers his hand to Freeman, they shake hands in a business-like manner.

> GEORGE
> Hey, man, if you've got something to say - you just gotta go out there and
> say it! Time is money, this is New York!

Freeman withdraws his hand and bids farewell.

EXT. WESTBROOK'S APARTMENT BUILDING - DAY

Children jump double-Dutch. Freeman lethargically opens the front door and enters. The huge ornate door closes.

FADE

INT. WESTBROOK'S PAD - DAY

Order has been restored. Freeman's stuff is piled neatly in a chair, his bed is made.

Westbrook is putting the finishing touches to a thorough reordering of creeping chaos. The mirror is sparkling, reflecting sunlight. The ceramic dish of change is no longer where it was.

> FREEMAN
> Man, I was gonna get all the stuff together today. Just this morning, I
> said, man, you gotta...

He stops mid-sentence as Westbrook SLAPS the *Downbeat* magazines on the table and drops the barbells PLONK in the corner. He calmly pulls a chair and sits directly in front of a gaping Freeman.

WESTBROOK

Freeman, I gotta talk to you, man. This fucking shit of you helping your-self to my tips has got to stop. You dig, man, it has got to come to an end!

FREEMAN

It was just a loan, man, I'll pay you back, with interest too, man, I'll get a job, man, I'll get a job … I'll …

WESTBROOK

Don't give me no jive bullshit, Freeman! You can accommodate yourself here. I can give you a place to sleep, I can give you a meal ticket. But, man, I can't provide for you. This is New York. (with compassion) You've got to make it for yourself! (silence.) I gotta go, see you later.

REACTION - Freeman

Dejection, compounded by the day's events. He sinks into the armchair and barely nods as Westbrook says good-bye.

WE HEAR STRAIGHTEN UP AND FLY RIGHT.

EXT. ACME EMPLOYMENT AGENCY BUILDING - DAY

A woman with an ill-tempered child leaves the building under Freeman's uncertain gaze.

He turns to look at the child and enters the building almost backwards.

INT. ACME EMPLOYMENT AGENCY WAITING ROOM - DAY

In the company of TWO BLACK MALES, Freeman thumbs through *Life* magazine. The younger man scans the bulletin board, covered with descriptions of placements for menial labor.

WE HEAR A WHITE FEMALE THICK BROOKLYN ACCENT summon a "MR MCKNIGHT" to the counter.

The older of the two males rises to the counter.

INT. ACME EMPLOYMENT AGENCY, RECEPTIONIST'S STATION - DAY

RECEPTIONIST
(patronizing)
So, come back next week and I think I'll have something for you.

Mr. McKnight turns and departs.

                          RECEPTIONIST
                (neck craned in direction waiting room)
            Well, young man, what can I do for you?

INT. ACME EMPLOYMENT AGENCY WAITING ROOM - DAY

Freeman, looks at the other male and then straight ahead as he realizes he is being addressed. He replaces the magazine on the table and walks towards the Receptionist's Station.

INT. ACME EMPLOYMENT AGENCY RECEPTIONIST'STATION – DAY

                            FREEMAN
            Oh, uh, I'm looking for a job. I'm a college graduate - I got a degree in
            Biology.

                          RECEPTIONIST
            Oh, is that so? Complete this form and bring it back to me.

INT. ACME EMPLOYMENT AGENCY WAITING ROOM - DAY

Freeman completes the form efficiently and approaches the receptionist's station.

INT. ACME EMPLOYMENT AGENCY RECEPTIONIST'S STATION - DAY

The Receptionist already has a card (a job specification) in hand. As she accepts the form, she speaks without looking at it.

                          RECEPTIONIST
                    (handing him the card)
            Oh, I've got a job for you. It's in sewing. It's on 12th and Broadway. Just
            ask for Mr. Landinski. Tell him, Mrs. D'Mato sent you specifically.

                            FREEMAN
            But, ma'am, I've never sewn in my life!

                          RECEPTIONIST
            You'll learn. You kidding? Piece a cake!

INT. FACTORY, SEWING SWEATSHOP - DAY

Freeman enters a classroom-like setting of sewing machines, WHIRRING AND TICK-TACKING IN TIME by 3-4 dozen workers, mostly middle-aged females.

The high ceilings ECHO THE DIN OF LABOUR. He walks tentatively towards the FOREMAN (LADINSKI), who paces work area like a sentinel.

Ladinski spins around quickly in response to Freeman's tap on his shoulder. He glowers at Freeman.

                    FREEMAN
          I am sorry to intrude, but Mrs. D'Mato asked me to say that she sent me
          specifically.

                    LANDISKI
                    (throaty accent)
          Very good. Very good. Seventy-five cents per hour. It is easy job. Overalls
          in locker room (pointing to end of the sewing area). MAUD show you.
          (bellowing) Maud! Maud! You come here!

In the background, a middle-aged female switches off her machine, wipes her brow and walks over, after muttering a sly remark to a colleague of similar age.

                    MAUD
                    (removing her gloves)
          Be right there, Mr Ladinski!

                    LADINSKI
          Put this young man - what's your name, son?

                    FREEMAN
          Freeman Lee.

                    LADINSKI
                    (confused)
          Put, uh, Lee here on number 2. Show him what to do, let him be safe.
          Can't have no more people sewing fingers on the machine. Needle is for
          pieces, not for the pinkies!

Laughing at his own macabre humor, Landinski turns his back, self-satisfied with his wit.

                    MAUD
          Yes, Mr. Ladinski. Hi, Freeman. It's real easy, pay no attention to him.
          That Ladinski's a goddamned fool, he works for the boss and he thinks
          he's God. Besides, he's as deaf as a coot! Can't hear a thing, poor fool.
          Too much yellin! (laughs)

Maud leads Freeman to Number 2 machine

MAUD

Where're you from, sonny? You ain't from New York, that's for sure!

FREEMAN

I'm from Ohio but I live at St. Nicholas Street now. I was born here too.

MAUD

Oh yeah? So, you got you a nice little ride home. An educated boy like you could read himself to death before that D train comes.

Maud picks up two pieces of cloth, puts them under the needle to demonstrate as she speaks.

Well, you just take this and stitch as straight as you can here to right about there… and when you've done that, you just take it and put it over there in ELLA'S box. This is Ella. (She gestures to Ella who nods as she counts pieces.) You just put it in Ella's box and forget about it. Then you do the next one. Dead simple. But stitch 'em straight, go real slow till you get the hang of it. (looks at Freeman and flashes a bawdy laugh.) The machine itself will go according to your rhythm and speed!

REACTION - Freeman

Awe at simplicity of sewing magazine, embarrassed at sexual innuendo from a woman old enough to be a friend of his grandmother. He sits down and takes up his position on the machine.

FADE

EXT. FACTORY - DAY

The main door opens and a queue of workers shuffle in and Freeman is among them.

INT. FACTORY - DAY

Freeman is engrossed in sewing. A clock on the wall makes it eleven fifty-nine.

INT. FACTORY LOCKER ROOM - DAY

MAUD

You hear 'bout that lynchin'? Don't know when all this is gonna end…

ELLA

My cousin, Mary-Louise, she came just yesterday from Mississipi. She said there's gonna be trouble! People're gonna turn against that, resist…

ANGLE on Freeman who enters, flops down on a bench, flips the straps of his overalls over his shoulders. With his overalls hanging about his waist, Freeman tilts his head back and closes his eyes.

Freeman goes into REVERIE. The drone of Maud and Ella's conversation DISSOLVES into SWING WITH A STRIDENT BRASS EMPHASIS.

ANGLE on Freeman's tired face, sharpening to a pout which says "This ain't nice work and I didn't want to get it"

DISSOLVE TO

REVERIE - COLLEGE DAYS - 1948 - BLACK AND WHITE

EXT. WILBERFORCE UNIVERSITY CAMPUS - DAY -1948

The well-kept campus grounds are set off by students *en route* to classes, strolling couples, study groups under trees and touch football games in progress.

INT. GYMNASIUM, WILBERFORCE CAMPUS, BASKETBALL COURT - DAY

A group of young men await the arrival of the coach. Some warm up, others chatter, some shoot baskets.

> FREEMAN
> Hey, cats, let's see some dunkin' the way coach doesn't like it – nice and crude! (assumes a shrill voice) "There's an art to shooting a basket, gentlemen."

A number of players appreciate Freeman's humour.

> BASKETBALL PLAYER #1
> While you're here dunkin' them baskets, someone else is dunkin' over at your NADINE'S!

Most players appreciate this comment but Freeman is visibly embarrassed.

INT. WILBERFORCE COLLEGE CAMPUS, SHORTER WOMEN'S DORMITORY, RECEPTION AREA - DAY

Freeman, still in basketball gear, exchanges a few words with the guard/housemother and signs in the visitors' book, checking his watch for the time. A sign displays – "Visiting Hours 14:00 – 18:30"

INT. WILBERFORCE UNIVERSITY SHORTER WOMEN'S DORMITORY CORRIDOR - DAY

Freeman raps gently at a door. The door opens to reveal NADINE, a beautiful woman with a sapodilla skin tone.

She opens the door fully to reveal a YOUNG MAN seated on a crumpled bed. Nadine and company are fully clad, if the clothing is a little bit crushed.

Freeman walks away.

INT. WILBERFORCE UNIVERSITY COLLEGIANS BAND ROOM - NIGHT

A band is in practice with a jazz standard. FRANK FOSTER leads the band, the trumpet section changes key. Freeman notices too late. Players stop, Freeman hears himself and stops.

LAUGHTER

                              FREEMAN
          Hey, man, you cats can't just keep changin' key on me like that. (Pouts.)
          Every night, every night.

The band resumes. On this occasion, Freeman adjusts to the surprise key change in time.

When he rests for the bass solo, Freeman smiles warmly - he is satisfied with his progress.

EXT. DESERTED COLLEGE CAMPUS - DAY

Freeman quickens his stroll, in an attempt to avoid an elderly gentleman, MR. CHARLES HILL, who is heading in an adjacent direction, but only succeeds in calling attention to himself.

Mr. Hill approaches him directly.

                              MR. HILL
          Mr. Lee, shouldn't you be elsewhere? Remember, this is the fifth year you
          have spent minoring your way around my campus. You would be well
          advised to take those nagging but necessary five credits, because I intend
          for you to graduate this spring!

                              FREEMAN
                       (with the charm of childhood)
          Oh, yes, Mr. Hill. I was just heading to the lab, sir. Need to see some,
          uh, dissected specimens.

Mr. Hill eyes him sceptically and walks on.

INT. WILBERFORCE UNIVERSITY COLLEGIANS BAND ROOM - DAY

WE HEAR STARDUST.

Frank creates a marvellous bop solo. Freeman creates a solo half way between swing and bop.

The tension with Frank is musically effective.

EXT. WILBERFORCE UNIVERSITY, COMMENCEMENT EXERCISES, 1949 - DAY

Proud families of the graduates gather to witness the culmination of the class of 1949's achievement of Bachelors' Degrees and listen intently to the President of the University.

The spectators wear their finest, with a female emphasis of stunning hats.

> MR. HILL
> And I take great pleasure in presenting to you, ladies and gentlemen,
> our class of 1949...LAMONT, Edgar Washington, LAVERNE, Susan
> Pamela, LEE Charles Freeman, LEE Jane Louise...

Among the queue of graduating students to receive their diplomas are a dignified, proud Jane Lee and a nonchalant (Charles) Freeman Lee.

ANGLE ON GRANDMOTHER MARY, FREEMAN'S FATHER and the rest of the LEES, applauding their Freeman and their Jane.

DISSOLVE TO

INT. FACTORY LOCKER ROOM - NIGHT

Freeman opens his eyes to an empty room. He removes his overalls, hangs them up and leaves.

INT. WESTBROOK'S APARTMENT - NIGHT

Westbrook enters to find Freeman dozing in an armchair, trumpet in hand.

> WESTBROOK
> (warm laugh)
> This is New York, buddy, work all day, can't play all night!

Freeman wakes up.

> FREEMAN
> Oh, hey, man. You want the good news or the bad news first?

> WESTBROOK
> Freeman, with you, I don't know, man. I just don't know. Good news
> could be bad news so let me have the bad news first.

FREEMAN
(rising)

The bad news is I lost my job. Through no fault of my own. The Landiski cat just came in and handed us our walking papers. Evidently the factory's gone bust. It was hard on some of the ladies. Anyway, the good news is that I got another job. I'm wrapping packages at Dwelling Homes.

Westbrook laughs, hands Freeman a beer.

WESTBROOK

So, when are you gonna play that trumpet, man?

FREEMAN

I don't know man. I wanted to get up on the bandstand tonight, but I was so beat after my, uh, dismissal, I just practiced at home.

WESTBROOK
(unconvinced, looks Freeman in the eye)

Oh? Hhmph, gets pretty rough here. You gotta work as a musician or you gotta wrap packages – like night and day. Night comes after day and day comes after night but I ain't never seen day and night together in one day?

FREEMAN
(chuckles)

Westbrook, you are a comedian, man. But, I, uh, I dig what you are cruisin' at.

WE HEAR NIGHT AND DAY.

FADE

EXT. NEW YORK CITY STREET, BUS STOP - DAY

Freeman runs towards a crowded rush-hour bus and just makes it.

INT. BUS [MOVING] - DAY

Freeman observes a man entering with a saxophone case. He is bleary eyed.

Their eyes meet and Freeman turns sharply to the window. He sheds a tear of envy and frustration.

INT. DWELLING HOMES DEPARTMENT STORE, HOME ACCESSORIES FLOOR - DAY

The store is busy. Decorations indicate the onslaught of the holiday season.

Freeman stands behind a counter marked 'PACKAGES' meticulously wrapping a lampshade for a CUSTOMER, a fur-coated lady with a hat very similar in shape to the shade.

He hands her the package, she thanks him.

INT. DWELLING HOMES, HOME ACCESSORIES FLOOR, METERS FROM THE EXIT - DAY

As the Customer walks towards the exit, her package begins to unravel.

She tries to grasp the paper, smiling to keep her dignity but the package comes apart and exposes the lampshade.

She allows the paper to fall and holding the bare lampshade she storms over the customer services counter.

From Freeman's viewpoint, ANGLE on:

The supervisor (MRS. DEVINE) and the customer converse, the former nodding knowingly and agreeably. Mrs. Devine lifts the receiver and accepts the lampshade from the customer.

INT. DWELLING HOMES, PACKAGES COUNTER - DAY

Freeman reaches for items from a customer, takes a box of glasses and gives a lampshade to his COLLEAGUE who accepts it, resentfully.

Mrs. Devine approaches.

> MRS. DEVINE
> Freeman, may I speak to you for a minute?

Freeman leaves the counter and approaches Mrs. Devine, while his colleague scowls in their direction. Freeman re-enters Packages Counter and gets his coat.

> FREEMAN
> (to perplexed colleague)
> Now your dream's come true, man. I'm splitting, I'm gonna be a mes-
> senger. Wrap 'em good, buddy, see ya!

INT. BUS - DAY

The saxophone player enters. He looks at Freeman and both acknowledge the futility of trying to converse in a crowded bus. The contact is satisfying.

INT. DWELLING HOMES MESSENGER STATION - DAY

Freeman enters, tentative. The SUPERVISOR rises, hands him a cap and jacket. Freeman dons the attire and making a mirror of the glass panel on a door, adjusts the cap to suit.

SUPERVISOR
(pins identification badge on Freeman's jacket)
You're right on target. There's a message at East Thirty Ninth and First.

EXT. WAREHOUSE BUILDING, VICINITY GRAND CENTRAL STATION - DAY

Freeman rings the bell.

WE HEAR THE SHRILL MUSICAL FEMALE VOICE 'WHO WOULD YOU LIKE TO SEE?'

FREEMAN

Messenger!

WE HEAR 'TAKE THE SIDE ENTRANCE, PLEASE'.

INT. WAREHOUSE - DAY

Freeman enters, steps over a few boxes towards a glass cubicle, takes an envelope from a man in conversation on the phone and departs. A clock above the man shows nine-thirty.

EXT. GRAND CENTRAL STATION, NEWSSTAND - DAY

Freeman, beaming ironically in his messenger uniform, strolls the streets amidst the hustle and bustle.

WE HEAR NICE WORK IF YOU CAN GET IT.

INT. GRAND CENTRAL STATION, NEWSSTAND - DAY

Freeman, among the sea of travellers, casually combs through the newspapers and *Downbeat*. Most papers lead with coverage of the Korean War. The odd back page story covers a lynching.

A clock on the wall above makes it ten forty-five.

Freeman continues to comb through the papers.

EXT. DWELLING HOMES DEPARTMENT STORE - DAY

Freeman quickens his pace to a run and enters.

INT. DWELLING HOMES MESSENGER DEPARTMENT - DAY

> MRS DEVINE
> (glowering)
> Mr. Lee, I'm beginning to think that you're just not <u>happy</u> here. So here!
> (She hands him an envelope.) I think I'm going to let you go where you
> can be <u>happy</u>!

She storms out.

CLOSE TO:

INT. PARADISE CLUB - NIGHT

The jam session is led by GEORGE NICHOLAS (BIG NICK).

Present are a mix of old and younger musicians: THELONIOUS MONK, ELMO HOPE, LESTER YOUNG, SONNY ROLLINS, DIZZY GILLESPIE, BENNY BAILEY, ART FARMER, IDRESS SULIEMAN, WILBUR HOGAN, JO GORDON and BLUE MITCHELL.

The session is swinging with DOODLIN'.

Freeman and DaCosta are seated in among patrons, rather than musicians. DaCosta's stare is intense.

> FREEMAN
> Man, you better watch out, man, or them eyeballs of yours're gonna roll
> over to the guitar player you're so busy staring at.

They laugh heartily as DaCosta relaxes. Freeman leans forward in his laugh and as he looks up, it freezes into a smile.

A few tables away, is seated JENNY in the company of two females.

Jenny is beautiful, exquisitely tasteful, an ethereal but all-pervasive presence. Jenny and Freeman make eye contact. She smiles deliberately, sweetly, coyly and casts her eyes down.

> DACOSTA
> Now your eyeballs gonna be droppin' out and rolling all the way over to
> that table. (laughs). I know her. She's married to MILT JACKSON, the
> vibraphone player.

> FREEMAN
> Oh, really? Wow, she's fine!

INT. LOBBY OF WESTBROOK'S APARTMENT BUILDING - NIGHT

Freeman cheerfully removes the mail, sees familiar handwriting, shakes the letter and smiles. He walks briskly up the stairs. WE HEAR I'VE GOT YOU UNDER MY SKIN.

INT. WESTBROOKS'S APARTMENT - NIGHT

Freeman opens the front door, tiptoes in, looks behind the space-maker and sees Westbrook's empty bed.

Freeman relaxes his steps, flicks on the lamp, takes a beer from the icebox and flops down in the armchair. He tears open the envelope to find another folded envelope.

INSERT - FOLDED ENVELOPE - "This came for you, Love, Grandma Mary." Freeman unfolds envelope.

INSERT - UNFOLDED ENVELOPE – "U.S. Govt. Draft Notice" addressed to Freeman in Ohio.

Freeman opens the seal, looks at the draft notice, throws it on the floor, angrily staring ahead. He paces, gets a second beer and closes his eyes. He laughs and sits down, looking straight ahead.

DISSOLVE TO

REVERIE - JAZZMEN AT WAR - 1950 -BLACK AND WHITE

EXT. OPEN FIELD - DAY

A big jazz band comprising Thelonious Monk, Dizzy Gillespie, Dacosta, Charley 'Bird' Parker, Miles Davis, Milt Jackson, Idrees Sulieman, Elmo 'Mo Hope, Jo Gordon, Blue Mitchell et. al., all dressed in military fatigues, play together. Suddenly, their respective instruments, perform a military function - Monk, Milt and Elmo receive and transmit morse code, guitars become guns and Freeman joins Blue Mitchell with a battle cry on bugle.

WE HEAR A HELICOPTER overhead. The men take cover, music scores are blown askew.

DISSOLVE TO

EXT. DAYTON CENTRAL TRAIN STATION PLATFORM - DAY

Freeman's friends, a trio, watch Freeman from the platform.

EXT. TRAIN, DAYTON CENTRAL TRAIN STATION - DAY

Freeman stands on the ledge of the carriage marked COLOREDS with an army green duffel bag on his shoulder.

FREEMAN

Hey, man, - gentlemen, fellow countrymen or whatever. (Laughs.) I'm telling you all, I'll be back in a few minutes, so hold my gig! Hold my trumpet too for that matter!

He throws his trumpet case underarm towards the trio.

EXT. DAYTON CENTRAL TRAIN STATION PLATFORM - DAY

Freeman's trumpet is caught with athletic skill by one of the trio, while in the background Freeman admires the catch.

FREEMAN

Don't think that'll be much good where I am headed. Try to keep her warm!

The trio laugh and the train inches away. Freeman is nowhere in sight.

INT. TRAIN [MOVING] AISLE – DAY

Freeman walks through the aisle, takes a seat in a carriage opposite a dark-brown male, with watery light brown eyes.

He appears to share Freeman's fate. He offers Freeman a cigarette. Freeman accepts.

FREEMAN

Hey, man, you about to go over there on that peninsula and get shot at? They're killing the United States over there!

STRANGER

No, way, brother. I don't wanna go but (nervous laugh) we're going anyway

FREEMAN

Man, I'm happy to go. I just know they won't be happy to have me! And I'll be happy to go home!

The laughter subsides, and the men withdraw into silence, contemplation.

INSERT - a sign "STATE OF KENTUCKY"

FREEMAN

You ever been to Kentucky?

STRANGER

No, man, I'm from a little town way up north, near Canada. Cleveland is the biggest town I've seen and this'll be my first time out of state.

FREEMAN

I went to Kentucky… a long time ago. To see my mother's people…they were share croppers. As a matter of fact, all my people are from Kentucky, except me and my sister. I was born in New York and she was born in Springfield, Ohio. I have absolutely no recollection of my mother…but I sure remember what it was like in Kentucky. (laughs) The outhouses that I remember real good - etched in the mind like a good composition! (He bursts into laughter.) But I never dreamed this would be my next Kentucky venture!

STRANGER joins in the laughter, clearly not sure of the source of humor.

Freeman looks out the window at the passing scenery.

DISSOLVE TO

REVERIE - FAMILY VISIT, KENTUCKY - 1933 - BLACK AND WHITE

INT. BACK SEAT OF A STATIONARY AUTOMOBILE - NIGHT

A six- year old Freeman asleep in the middle of the backseat opens his eyes and looks forward between the two front seats of the vintage Ford. He sees a figure in the distance with a flickering lantern.

EXT. DESERTED TRAIL FLANKED BY OPEN FIELDS IN RURAL KENTUCKY - NIGHT

BILL approaches the completely dark scene with the surefooted gait of rural life, guided only by the low beam of the automobile's lights and his lantern.

WE HEAR CRICKETS, FROGS, OWLS AND OTHER CREATURES OF THE NIGHT.

Freeman's father and his sisters search the darkness for the flicker of the lantern held out to the side of the approaching figure. JANE takes hold of her father's hand.

MARY

Freeman, you'd better wake up or your eyes gonna get glued together. Blaah! (sticks her tongue out)

INT. AUTOMOBILE - NIGHT

Freeman shows signs of life and with great effort leans over, unlocks the car door and scampers out, bleary-eyed but pretended not to be.

EXT. DESERTED TRAIL IN RURAL KENTUCKY - NIGHT

The dark scene is now illuminated by the approaching lantern, casting shadows over the faces of the three children, Mr. Lee and Bill, its bearer. He is the brother of Freeman's late mother.

Freeman darts around the car towards Bill and the others, stumbles and falls.

Mary rushes to help him and Freeman cries in a low monotone, more embarrassed than hurt. Bill lifts him into the air.

> BILL
> So, Little Freeman, you're a big one, heavy (exaggerating). I hear you're doing real well in school. That's good, son, I am proud of you. Shooting up into the air like a quick growing corn. (holding Freeman way up above his head)

Freeman squeals in delight.

> BILL
> (lowers Freeman to the ground)
> You look like your mama, boy, oh boy, you're the spittin, image of your mama.

INT. BEDROOM OF A RUSTIC HOUSE - DAY

His sisters asleep in bed, Freeman alone in a cot, opens his eyes, gets up with excitement.

He makes great effort pulling his clothes from the suitcase, of which he can unlock one buckle-fastener.

INT. RUSTIC KITCHEN - DAY

Freeman stands on tiptoes in an unsuccessful attempt to shift the bolt across the large handmade door.

Frustrated, his eyes wander around the kitchen and he climbs on the table and scampers through the window.

EXT. BACKYARD, SIDE SCENE OF POOR SHARECROPPERS RESIDENCE - DAY

Hens and chickens stare as Freeman lands on his backside and rolls over to rise.

He goes towards some furry baby chickens.

Fascinated, he puts some stealth in his pace. The hen pecks at him and he withdraws his little hand, astonished.

FADE TO

EXT. KENTUCKY COUNTRYSIDE, FORT KNOX - DAY

A bus trundles down a roadway leading to the entrance of an army base, flanked by two camouflage-painted tanks.

INT. FORT KNOX, DRAFTEES CHECKPOINT - DAY

Freeman approaches a desk where an OFFICER awaits. He is ageless, spectacled with a generous, liberal expression.

In the background, soldiers attend to routine matters for newcomers. There is morose murmuring about rations, combat units, supplies.

>   OFFICER
>   Sit down.

>   FREEMAN
>   I regret to inform you, but I don't really think you're really going to need
>   someone like me in your army. Man, I'm a musician and I don't know
>   anything about guns and shit.

REACTION - OFFICER

The ageless face of the Officer crumples into a brief frown, then with a twinkling of the eyes behind his glasses, he speaks with untoward courtesy, military over social etiquette.

>   OFFICER
>   Mr. Lee, Mr. Lee, you will be quiet this minute and answer my questions
>   as I ask. (reinforces sternness with a peek over his glasses). Is your name
>   Charles Freeman Lee?

>   FREEMAN
>   Yes, it is, but everyone calls me Freeman. If you call me Charles, I am liable
>   not to answer because I'll think you're talking to that guy over there.

Freeman points to a young crew-cut white soldier in the background.

>   OFFICER
>   Mr. Lee, you are here to be enlisted of the services of United States Army
>   and you <u>will</u> answer with some regard to relevance.

FREEMAN

I told you I'm a musician and I play the trumpet. And a little piano too.
As a matter of fact...

OFFICER

(interrupting)
Is your date of birth 13 August 1927?

FREEMAN

Yes, it is. But Chuck? You can forget that too.

REACTION Officer - Perplexed but intrigued.

FREEMAN

You know, Charles from Chuck?

REACTION Officer

The Officer inhales deeply, blows a whistle to summon help as his neck and lower jaw stiffen in military rigor.

TWO SOLDIERS approach Freeman.

SOLDIER#1

Please remove your watch and empty your pockets.

OFFICER

I am confining you to secure accommodation.

CLOSE TO

INT. FORT KNOX ARMY NUTHOUSE - NIGHT

The inmates are in varying stages of strangeness and rebellion. There much chatter, argumentative tones and eerie laughter.

Freeman surveys the scene from a bench in the corner where he reads, glancing around furtively from time to time. He rises, looks around nervously and moves to explore the premises.

INT. FORT KNOX ARMY NUTHOUSE DORMITORY - NIGHT

An austere darkish room with bunk beds and tables set up as if for a wedding banquet look out through a window at a leafless tree. Freeman enters the room and looks around horror struck.

> FREEMAN
> (to himself)
> Man, they want me to sleep all night in here with these crazy cats. They've gotta be kidding! I want me a private room before they make me into Private Lee.

He makes his way to the far end of the room and goes through the door.

INT. FORT KNOX, ARMY NUTHOUSE, DARK CORRIDOR - NIGHT

Freeman moves tentatively through the corridor, picks a door at random and knocks politely. He pulls his hand away as a muffled but violent thumping is the response.

> VOICE
> Yessirree, captain, you can let me out of here now! I found the map, sir! It is slightly decrepit, sir, but we can read it and find the treasure, sir, lots of gold and diamond necklaces, sir, no skulls or bones, sir, just nice shiny things your wife might like to have. Yessirree, I found the map sir! Let me out! Let me out!

The door RATTLES with renewed thumping.

Freeman, completely aghast, turns around to come face to face with an army man in a white coat (ATTENDANT).

> FREEMAN
> Hey, uh, excuse me, sir… but I can't stay out there with those cats there, man, maybe I could have a padded cell…

> ATTENDANT
> Sorry, buddy, but, somehow, I just don't think you're crazy enough…

FADE

SUPER:

1993
THE INTERVIEW

EXT. PARIS, THE SEINE, VICINITY NOTRE DAME CATHEDRAL - NIGHT

ANGLE ON a *bateau-mouche* heading for the arc of lights on a bridge.

The Notre Dame cathedral is in background.

WE HEAR MUSIC

FADE

INT. LE BAISER SALE JAZZ CLUB, PARIS - DAY

Freeman and the Interviewer are seated at a table in the unusual atmosphere of an empty jazz club in the mid-afternoon.   Freeman is behind the long table, covered in a white table cloth.

The Interviewer sits on the other side and is only partially reflected in a large framed mirror hanging behind Freeman.

WE HEAR A SELECTION FROM THE DIAL SESSIONS.

THE INTERVIEWER

You were telling me about the school band – seventh grade?

FREEMAN

Oh, wow! My contribution to the school band? Nil! My music teacher made me play a duet with a <u>girl</u>. And so, the day we were supposed to do it – all the other kids out there - my sister was playing a duet with somebody - and so I left my music at home, so she is not going to make me play it.

But she made me get up and play it anyway and I just messed up. You see that leaves scars on little kids. That must account for my erratic behaviour now! (laughs)

I was interested in basketball. I was a physical ed. major when I first got into college…oh, yeah, sure… something happened.

My girlfriend and I split up and uh…No, no, I was going out for basketball, but I could not go out for basketball because visiting hours was at the same hours basketball practice was, right, so…

THE INTERVIEWER

Visiting hours for what?

FREEMAN

She lived in a dormitory! Right? Visiting hours were a certain time in the dormitory! And that's the same time basketball practice was and so they, so they told me some other guy was going over there during visiting hours - so I just had to miss basketball! (laughs).

So, I went out one day and that was the day they were cutting the team, so they cut me right off the team with everyone else. I didn't care.

So then, then I said well, maybe, I could start to play but I couldn't even make the band - Wilberforce Collegians. I couldn't read. I was pitiful really, I didn't know how to read.

So, I played like Roy Eldridge. Frank was there, them cats were playing bebop shit, you know.

Frank Foster was there. He was with Count Basie, he's leading the band now.

THE INTERVIEWER

Was this a black school?

FREEMAN

Yes, one of the all black schools. There's Wilberforce, Tuskegee, Howard, Tennessee State, Alabama A & M, Alcorn, Grambling, Prairie View. A bunch of 'em and Wilberforce was just one them. But Wilberforce had Wilberforce Collegians and a bunch of musicians came out of Wilberforce – Benny Carter, Ben Webster ... no not Ben Webster – Billy Strayhorn, and a bunch of people played in Wilberforce Collegians. I got a book at home if you want a list. Freeman Lee!

THE INTERVIEWER

Charles Freeman Lee? What year did they cut you from the team?

FREEMAN

Freshman - I made the team in high school! I wasn't fooling around with girls. (laughs.) I was an athlete, didn't smoke, drink, do anything.

A broken heart and look what happened!

You see, I stayed in college for five years 'cause I was trying to make a career out college, but, uh, the Dean of Men knew me from when I was a little boy. He said he was going to kick me out anyway. After my fourth year, he said this is your last year, Freeman.

'Cause I had all my hours, you had to have, I think, fifty-five hours of Biology. I had fifty. I just wouldn't take that other five 'cause I have a minor in English, I have a minor in, uh, I have a whole lotta minors 'cause I was just minoring everything! (laughs)

I have an art minor. That class you just attend and you get a grade… and boy, I attended regularly! (laughs).

Boy, it seems really silly the things that you do when you haven't got any sense.

And most of the time when you're young and dumb - you know everything!

THE INTERVIEWER
Who else was in the band, this Wilberforce Collegians?

FREEMAN
Some of the guys who were on Collegian Band? Some of them were veterans who came back from World War II. We had veterans in the band. Yeah, these cats were <u>old</u> cats, 24 and 25 years old.

Well I don't know if you ever heard of Ernie Wilkins, he wrote the arrangement for '*Every Day*' for Count Basie, but his brother was there – Jimmy. The rest, nobody else took up music. Me and Frank were the only two who did music as a living.

Yeah, my school was famous for… George Russell was there. Ever heard of George Russell? He wrote music for Dizzy's world tour for American goodwill, (laughs) in 1956. You know, Cubano Be, Cubano Bop and whatever!

He was there. He was in the tenth grade with me but George must have been about four or five years older than me. (laughs.) He didn't do nothing anyway.

George is a good-looking guy. I don't know what he did in high school – he just came here now and then I think! And uh, a girl that sang with Duke Ellington – Joya Sherrill. She was in my graduating class.

THE INTERVIEWER
From Wilberforce University?

FREEMAN
From high school! I didn't know who was in my college graduating class except my sister. She caught up with me – she finished in three years, I finished in five. And she and I graduated at the same time.

THE INTERVIEWER
She is a teacher in Ohio now?

FREEMAN

Yeah, she teaches. She is a professor. She teaches at Wilberforce University for that matter, she and her husband Wilfred Ball. A whole lotta guys came out of Wilberforce Collegians. I can make a list for you if you want.

Wilberforce and, uh, Alabama A & M., they turned out some good musicians. Wilberforce, Alabama and Tennessee State were turning out some good musicians. Most cats don't go college, that's the thing. At Wilberforce, they let guys come

FREEMAN (CONT'D)

there as special students, you know. But, uh, I got a degree, of course. In Biology, of course.

Music just seemed out of the question! (laugh)

THE INTERVIEWER

So, you didn't bother to study music?

FREEMAN

Music, I didn't take any music in college except... guys used to pick on me all the time. You see Frank and I was cool. Frank knew everything!

I mean as a 13 or 14 year-old kid he could write for a whole band! Frank, Frank was a phenomenally talented cat! Frank Foster, yeah.

Uh, the new Charlie Parker record come out - Swingmatism? Frank come over to my house and put the record on, get a piece of paper and just write it right down. No piano! No anything! What key man?! He'd write it all down. He was an extremely talented cat!

I never aspired to be a Frank Foster. In a jam session? Okay!

But I mean as an all-round musician he was, uh, he is excellent!

But I could get him in a session. (laughs.) If you mean creativity, you know that's two different things. At least I would like to think I can, get him I mean.

THE INTERVIEWER

But you said when he was 13 he could write music?

FREEMAN

Oh, I, I knew Frank before he came to school. He had a big band. Billy Brooks wasn't in it, I don't think 'cause I think Billy was gone by then.

But Billy can tell you that Frank had a band when he was 13 or 14 years old. A big band and he wrote the arrangements.

He was a phenomenal talent! Frank Foster. He was a really a phenomenal little cat!   I am getting there!

THE INTERVIEWER

Where?

FREEMAN

Wherever it is that I am supposed to be going! (laughs)

Frank is from Ohio, Billy Brooks is from Ohio, George Russell is from Ohio, Benny Bailey is from Ohio, Billy Strayhorn is from Ohio, a lotta cats that I probably could name... Snooky Young was with, uh, that Johnny Carson show - Doc Severinsen's band? He has been there about 20 years. Before that he was with Count Basie. He was with Lionel Hampton, too I believe, 'cause he can play real high too. All those guys went to school in Dayton....

FADE TO

EXT. THE OWL CLUB, DAYTON, OHIO - NIGHT

A periods poster advertises a performance by Snooky Young's band with Freeman on piano, JOHNNY LYTLE on drums, EDDIE 'LOCKJAW' DAVIS on saxophone, special guest SLAM STEWART on bass. Finely attired would-be patrons stand in a slow-moving queue.

INT. BANDSTAND, THE OWL CLUB - NIGHT

The band nears the end of a standard - MEAN TO ME - with a swing emphasis.

Freeman's piano solo, distinctly bop ('hip shit') shows tension with the drummer, at whom Freeman glances austerely from time to time.

SNOOKY

Ladies and gentlemen, I'd like to introduce the members of my band. On drums - Johnny Lytle.

Lytle begins to rat-tat-tat and Freeman cuts in with a quick double chord improvisation. Snooky smiles at the tension and continues.

> SNOOKY
> Our saxophone man is Eddie "Lockjaw" Davis, and a special welcome for Mr. Slam Stewart on bass.

The audience applauds.

> SNOOKY (CONT'D)
> And I pay a special welcome to our piano man, Freeman Lee, who just came back from an all expenses vacation with Uncle Sam. And I am Snooky Young!

Lytle gives an ironic drumroll. The band members laugh uproariously as do some members of the audience. The entire band joins the finale.

The mainly black audience applauds.

> SNOOKY
> Right now, we're gonna take a break. The bar is open!

INT. BAR, OWL CLUB - NIGHT

The bar, adjacent to the bandstand, is extremely busy as musicians await the BARMAN who, with a female assistant, beautifully clad, tries to keep up with the frenetic pace of intermission orders.

> FREEMAN
> (leans over and directs speech in Barman's face)
> I want me six double vodkas.

> BARMAN
> Six double vodkas?

> FREEMAN
> Man, have you got a problem hearing or something? This is a bar, right? You must've seen me playing here every night, right? Well then, yeah, I wanna have me six double vodkas.

> BARMAN
> Man, I heard you. (to Snooky.) What you cats been doin' to my man?

SNOOKY
(laughs at the fury of Freeman)
Freeman here thinks he is the hippest thing in the band, playing all this hip shit…

FREEMAN
(gathering together his six double vodkas)
Man, I dig hip shit! And want to play hip shit - and I do or at least I try to. I am just tired of this drummer cat, man, rat-tat-tat-ing through my solos. Every night, every night, rat-tat-tat, rat-tat-tat, brr brr, brr brr… (raises the first of the vodkas) Man, I am gonna set those drums on fire!

SNOOKY
(humours the rage of Freeman, touching his shoulder)
You're gonna do what?

FREEMAN
(taking a second double vodka)
You heard me, Snooky! (empties glass in one swill.) I'm gonna set those drums ablaze when I get back there on that bandstand!

REACTION - COMPANY

Laughter.

EXT. THE OWL CLUB, DAYTON OHIO - DAY

A period poster advertises CANDY JOHNSON'S BAND, JACK MCDUFF (piano) JAMES GLOVER (bass) DON VENDERS (drums) ED "MOON" MULLENS (tenor sax).

A drum kit, bass and props are being moved in by a crowd of four. McDuff supervises the operation, holding the door open with his foot.

INT. THE OWL CLUB, DAYTON OHIO - DAY

The afternoon suns seeps in through high ventilation slats just below the ceiling, bathing the otherwise stale atmosphere of an empty nightclub with rays of light, criss-crossing Candy, Glover, Venders and Freeman who are at a table eating.

Moon sits alone, huddled over and in shivery discomfort. Heads turns in unison as the CLATTER of moving instruments beckons.

WE HEAR CRISSCROSS

INT. FOYER, BANDSTAND, THE OWL CLUB, DAYTON, OHIO - DAY

The full blast of daylight streams into the club as McDuff throws open the interior double doors with majesty.

The men finish eating, the chatter ceases and Glover and Venders get up and help McDuff with setting up the bandstand.

INT. THE OWL, DAYTON, OHIO - DAY

                    CANDY
So, yeah, Freeman, come with me on trumpet, man. We got gigs in Philly, we got gigs in New York.

                    FREEMAN
Gigs in, New York? Hey, man, what would bring you to little ol' Dayton?

                    CANDY
Okay, Freeman, okay, just gimme a break. Okay we got gigs in the New York area. We already got McDuff on piano – he keeps tellin' us he's gonna really get into organ but, uh, I have really only seen McDuff play with another organ…regularly! (laughs) So anyway, we got ourselves a piano man till McDuff plays another organ but, uh, we just ain't got nobody on trumpet – go with Moon, man, Moon's a bad tenor player!

                    FREEMAN
Wow! Man, sounds like you're makin' me an offer I can't refuse. But, uh, Snooky's bad trumpet player! But, unfortunately, I don't play with him in the band because he is playin' trumpet and I'm playin' piano… but I don't know … for one thing, Snooky is steady, he's based here, as a matter of fact he was born here man, I can't see how I can do better than that. Can I or are you trying to tell me I can?

                    CANDY
Freeman, man, you're a jive, man, a real jiveass. I tell you what - tonight I'll give you a guest appearance (hands Freeman a small roll of bills) and if you dig it, then you do, if you don't then you can't say I didn't give you a break.

FADE

INT. BANDSTAND, THE OWL DAYTON, OHIO - NIGHT

WE HEAR the gig in the full swing with CHEROKEE.

Freeman, relentless with sharp strident notes, forces the members of the band down for the solo. He shows off his key changes in improvisation.

McDuff gently embellishes his effort. The audience applauds. Freeman takes a bow, and the band resumes to the end of number.

INT. THE OWL CLUB, DAYTON, OHIO - NIGHT

A middle-aged couple clean up after the evening patrons, as the band members drink, smoke, talk shop, and laugh. Freeman, seated at the table by himself still jams on his horn.

> CANDY
>
> So, we gotta make room for one more in these automobiles. I think Freeman's gonna come with us. (hand over mouth) You gonna gig with us, right Freeman?

> MCDUFF
> (kidding around)
>
> Yeah, man, soon everybody's gonna be talkin' 'bout that bad trumpet player from Dayton – he's bad, can play his ass off, blowin' everybody away. Whatchya sayin' Freeman, my man?

Freeman removes his trumpet from his lips and bursts into laughter.

> FREEMAN
>
> I just started to cook, man. And I'm gonna be cooking till it starts to burrrn! But, uh, you know, I gotta split, gotta get some rest seeing as how I'm gonna have to sit between these two for the rest of the trip…

> MOON
> (fearful)
>
> But, Freeman, you're new man, you can't get the window seat, man, I've been here before you, man, you can't get a window seat before me, man.

> CANDY
> (impatient)
>
> Just listen to this asshole, fighting 'bout window seats and we ain't gone nowhere yet. (stares at the shivering Moon.) Yeah, Freeman, we're gonna go to Philly, little town in Maryland just outside of D.C. and New Jersey. The Jersey gig's good bread - lotta white assholes pay good money every now and then, place always full, you know, jumpin', full to the brim.

FREEMAN
I'll be ready, to go. Window seat or not. I just gotta see Snooky tomorrow
and tell him I am gonna split.

FADE

INT. BANDSTAND OF THE BACK OLIVE, SMALL TOWN, NEW JERSEY - NIGHT

Candy's band - Freeman, McDuff, Glover, Venders and Moon - wraps up a performance with THE SONG IS YOU,
with a spectacular range of improvisations.

INT. THE BLACK OLIVE, SMALL TOWN, NEW JERSEY - NIGHT

The audience, white and appreciative, applauds warmly.

INT. BANDSTAND OF THE BLACK OLIVE, SMALL TOWN, NEW JERSEY - NIGHT

The band members come forward to bow and as they retreat, the lights fade, instruments are removed, and they file
through the side of the stage.

EXT. STAGE EXIT, THE BLACK OLIVE, SMALL TOWN, NEW JERSEY - NIGHT

The band members file out of the club and head for their cars on the opposite side of the street.

WE HEAR MUSIC.

McDuff steps out into the street.

Out of nowhere, a car emerges from a side street, speeds towards him and SCREECHES to a halt, within inches in
his feet.

McDuff, looks astonished at others who take a few discreet steps in retreat, all the better to observe three white males
guffawing in the car.

McDuff unsticks his feet and runs to his car, frantically trying to open the driver's door.

WE HEAR LAUGHTER as the car drives away with SCREECHING TYRES.

FREEMAN
(shouting)
McDuff, you know an after-hours place man, we've gotta get off these
streets. This New Jersey is like the wild west!

                              MCDUFF
                         (cathartic laugh)
              Yeah, man, I know a joint. Let's check it out.

INT. THE BROWN DERBY, SMALL TOWN, NEW JERSEY - NIGHT

In a dingy but atmospheric afterhours club, Freeman and Moon play, barely visible on the small bandstand while the others drink, smoke, talk, and socialize.

McDuff and Candy get up and leave with female company. Freeman and Moon continue to play rich warm notes which linger in the wisps of smoke, filtered by the coloured light bulbs.

INT. ENTRANCE OF THE BROWN DERBY, SMALL TOWN NEW JERSEY - NIGHT

In walks a buxom WHITE FEMALE on the arm of a MAN, a snazzy dresser, evidently well-known, as a flurry of sibilant greetings follow the entrance of the couple.

WE HEAR 'HEY, PORKCHOPS, MY MAN' from selected sycophants in the audience.

Porkchops leads his lady to a table.

WE HEAR AN ABRUPT STOP OF THE SAXOPHONE, THE TRUMPET CONTINUES.

INT. BANDSTAND, THE BROWN DERBY, SMALL TOWN, NEW JERSEY - NIGHT

Moon has stopped playing and is clearly irritated by this small-town celebrity, Porkchops.

                              MOON
              Hey, who is that nigger with that fucking fat, very fucking ugly white
              broad? Man, you gonna cross the color line, get it fine - not fucking
              weighing nine hundred and ninety- fucking-nine!!

INT. THE BROWN DERBY, SMALL TOWN, NEW JERSEY - NIGHT

                            PORKCHOPS
              Who you callin' fat, piece of shit jazzboy?

INT. BANDSTAND, THE BROWN DERBY, SMALL TOWN, NEW JERSEY - NIGHT

Freeman runs a whole line of high notes, picks up the tempo in a vain attempt to diffuse the impending confrontation.

MOON
Boy, I'll talk about your mama, y'hear, I'll talk about your Mama!

FREEMAN
Moon, you're a dumb-assed piece of shit, man! You have got to see that we're outnumbered! Just ease on outta the joint... look there is a side door. Quit looking at me, asshole, just move, quick, ease on outta here!

INT. AUDIENCE, THE BROWN DERBY, SMALL TOWN, NEW JERSEY - NIGHT

PORKCHOPS
I'll shoot your motherfucking face in, boy...

EXT. SIDE EXIT, THE BROWN DERBY, SMALL TOWN, NEW JERSEY - NIGHT

Freeman and Moon move a garbage can behind the door and run.

EXT. ALLEY, VICINITY THE BROWN DERBY SMALL TOWN, NEW JERSEY- NIGHT

WE HEAR THE TUMBLE AND CLANKING of a garbage can and the FOOTSTEPS of Freeman and Moon, running down the alley. They accelerate as gunshots ring out in the darkness.

A cab pulls up at the end of the alley, headlights on Freeman and Moon. McDuff jumps out of the front seat.

MOON
(shouting breathlessly)
Jesus god, McDuff, some cat' s up there in the alley shootin' at us - you got your gun?

MCDUFF
(walking slowly and bellowing the conk out of his hair)
Yeah, I've got my gun! Why?

EXT. ALLEY, THE BROWN DERBY 'S SIDE EXIT, SMALL TOWN, NEW JERSEY - NIGHT

WE HEAR THE CLATTER of a garbage can and FOOTSTEPS of Porkchops and two others.

They suddenly turn and run in the opposite direction, back towards the Brown Derby.

INT. CAB [MOVING] A STREET, VICINITY THE BROWN DERBY, SMALL TOWN, NEW JERSEY - NIGHT

                    FREEMAN
McDuff, you ain't got shiiit, right? I mean I ain't never seen you with no gun.

                    MCDUFF
Yeah, I ain't got shiit. I never held a gun since the day I left Illinois!

REACTION COMPANY- LAUGHTER

INT. HOTEL ROOM, SMALL TOWN, NEW JERSEY - NIGHT

Moon, Glover, Venders and Freeman listen intently as McDuff holds court.

                    MCDUFF
Look, man, I mean it - Candy just aint treatin' us right! Three nights in a row and the place was jumping, filling up to the brim – and what do we get from Candy? The same old shit that we get for a gig in fuckin' no place, Colorado. He just aint doin' it – them club managers, I see'em – all grinnin' and smilin' that shit-eatin' grin when they see the cash flowing in. They laid good bread on Candy!

                    MOON
That's right. You're right, McDuff. I mean Candy ain't never gave me a raise and I stayed with him when I could have gone with…

                    MCDUFF
Shit, Moon, you'd shoot every extra dime he gave you then get sick when it's all gone! Maybe you helped to fuck everything up – you're always high and shit, raggedy clothes. And we ain't got no money! Candy takes one look at your raggedy shit and he thinks we can all wear raggedy shit. Fuck you, Moon!!

                    FREEMAN
Be cool, McDuff, shit, take it easy. Just chill. You're mad at Candy not at Moon – he's the one talkin' to the managers. (laughs.) He's our intermediary, the middle man.

                    DON VENDERS
But Candy works, man, them white cats ain't lay no extra bread on him. I know Candy is cool man…

MCDUFF

Candy is cool? You ain't know shit! That night at the Brown Derby, when Freeman and this asshole, Moon, nearly got shot by a bunch of cats because of this motor mouth here, me and Candy went with them sisters and I know from what my little lady said - Candy was layin' it on thick with his little woman. He's there pumpin' his lion's share of our money into some woman and me, I am there like a real asshole, can't lay any bread on the lady! Can't buy a spread, and good drink – can't buy shit on this nickel and dime shit Candy's payin'!

FREEMAN

So what d'you wanna do – split?

MOON

Yeah, yeah, McDuff, lets split, let's split. Let's me, and you and Freeman and Venders? (looking at Venders intently for slightest sign of disloyalty)

The door bursts open and Candy walks in, lipstick all over his face and shirt. Silence falls over the room.

CANDY

So, McDuff, you're not happy with the deal man? Don't dig it or you just beating your fuckin' ugly fat little gums together because you can't gig the chicks you want on what you make? If you can't dig it, jump off the wagon, McDuff. If you don't like it... them managers tell me that the minute my back's turned after a hard night's work you're busy talkin' real nice to them...

MCDUFF

Candy, you're a motherfucker, you know, man a real cocksuckin' motherfucker! You get extra bread laid on you all the time and you'd piss on it first before you'd pass some of it on down the line.

CANDY

Look, asshole, this is my gig. It's my gig, my ship – if you don't like it the way the captain's runnin' the ship – jump overboard, motherfucker.

MCDUFF

Moon, Freeman, lets split and go make our own bread.

CANDY

Well I got it. I can dig it. Venders you stayin' on board? So just fuck off you three – ain't stayin' in this shithole – I got myself a nice warm bed and company. Good fuckin' luck, it's been nice knowin' you.

Candy leaves the room, the door slamming passively behind him.

ANGLE ON the reflection of the trio in the window

INT. HOTEL ROOM, SMALL TOWN, NEW JERSEY - DAY

The mutinous threesome drink and smoke over a game of poker, the chips favour McDuff. Freeman folds his hand and takes a long swill of his vodka.

FREEMAN

McDuff, let's just be real, man, it's been six weeks and we got, what? Five gigs? Enough to keep us here payin' for this shithole?! Here's what I'm sayin' – I say after the next gig we just, you know, split up, go our own way.

MCDUFF

Alright, Freeman, so you wanna cut out? I saved your poor-assed life that night at the Brown Derby and now, two fuckin' hallelujahs later…

FREEMAN

Fuck you and the Brown Derby, McDuff! That was ages ago and you didn't even have no gun… talkin' 'bout you saved my little poor-assed life…

MCDUFF

So, what if I didn't have no gun? Them cats that was runnin' down the alley and shootin' at you didn't know that. I looked like I got one and that's what it takes! Look, man, the bread's gonna roll in, I'm gonna roll in it, I'm gonna play my ass off, wipe everybody out! Man, I'm gonna get real big, large, and gigs'll be comin' in… just stick around, Freeman.

FREEMAN

McDuff, here's the deal - you find three one-nighters in a row and I'll stay. If you don't, then the bread from the next gig's carfare to New York. Look, man, I'm telling you straight. I cut out on Snooky to go with Candy. You cut out Candy, no we cut out on Candy to go with you. Now I wanna cut loose, man. There's a lotta bad trumpet players around.

REACTION McDuff – dejection quickly masked by self-deprecating laughter.

FREEMAN

You got Stanley Turrentine, Art Farmer… you got a lotta bad trumpet players around… Or maybe you can learn to play organ like you keep tellin' us…

> ### MCDUFF
> Shit, Freeman, you just don't think I got it, huh? Shiit. Yeeahh. Shiiit. You gonna see what it's like when the bread starts rollin' in rolls and loaves, and then (inhales fiercely) it's gonna be just the raw dough...

REACTION COMPANY - LAUGHTER

CLOSE TO

EXT. WESTBROOK'S APARTMENT BUILDING, HARLEM - DAY

Freeman approaches with a confident saunter, an olive-green duffle bag on his shoulder.

He watches the little girls jump double-Dutch.

He stops in front of the door, removes his trumpet case from the bag, rests it on his thigh, and opens it. Trumpet raised to the building, Freeman blows a ripple of high notes.

EXT. THIRD FLOOR WINDOW OF WESTBROOK'S APARTMENT BUILDING. HARLEM, NEW YORK - DAY

Westbrook, leans out, his undershirt revealing firm biceps. He waves and grins warmly.

> ### WESTBROOK
> You're finally playin' that thing!

EXT. WESTBROOK'S APARTMENT BUILDING, HARLEM - DAY

Freeman opens the huge ornate door to a darkened lobby. He enters the building and the door slams.

INT. WESTBROOK'S APARTMENT BUILDING, HARLEM, - DAY

Freeman is seated in the armchair. Westbrook opens two bottles of beer and pours them simultaneously into two glasses, laughing heartily.

> ### FREEMAN
> No, no, man, Westbrook, this time I'm gonna do it! I know I didn't do nothing last time - I dunno. George just took me to see a bunch of white cats. But I'm ready now, man. You'll see.

> ### WESTBROOK
> Okay, Freeman, (handing him beer) let's drink to your arrival in New York - big time hip shit coming at you!

FREEMAN
(raising his glass, wet eyed and sentimental)
To friendship, man, to friendship.

WESTBROOK
So, Smitty's got the room nextdoor - we opened up the door to the kitchen so we just kinda have more room, use up the space. He's up in Tarrytown most of the time. He's usually here on weekends when you'll probably be working - till you meet up with that fine lady who came here looking for you last spring!

FREEMAN
What fine lady?

WESTBROOK
Real fine. Said her name was Jenny.

FREEMAN
Black hair, all pulled up on top, (gesticulates with sweep of hand over-head) like, kinda mellow skin, fine clothes, eyes wet and dreamy?

WESTBROOK
Oohh, so you know her?

FREEMAN
Yeah, I know her, but I didn't know her name was Jenny.

INT. BANDSTAND, PARADISE NIGHTCLUB, HARLEM - NIGHT

Four trumpeters – Freeman, Art Farmer, Benny Bailey and BLUE MITCHELL run through the bridge of Body and Soul in all keys as BIG NICK (GEORGE NICHOLAS) is at the controls.

The fourth trumpet player (Blue Mitchell) sits out the run of notes and he instead pats on his apparently stuck keys to release them.

BIG NICK
E flat!

The bridge is played in E flat.

BIG NICK
D flat!

The bridge is played in D flat

BIG NICK

B flat

The bridge is played in B flat

BIG NICK

E minor

The bridged played in E minor

BIG NICK

Okay, the tune is written in E natural so let's play it that way. (sotto voce)
Now that we know who's who in bop!

The band joins the trumpeters at the end of the bridge, and Blue Mitchell's keys suddenly become unstuck - he joins in too.

INT. 'MUSICIANS CORNER' PARADISE NIGHTCLUB, HARLEM - NIGHT

Thelonious Monk, Benny Bailey, Idrees Sulieman, Art Farmer, Sonny Rollins, Elmo Hope, Blue Mitchell, Joe Gordon are all sitting at a table in 'musicians' corner' among the audience. They talk shop.

MONK

Freeman, they've got a bad trumpet player from Delaware, name's Clifford
Brown. He can play his ass off, he's blowin' everybody away!

FREEMAN

Blow me away? You're puttin' me on, right? Man, I can hold my own!
Bring him on down here and I'll show him up! (laughs)

BENNY

So, Freeman, you're looking to work? Jo Lawson told me that Eddie
Vinson's lookin' for a trumpet player…

FREEMAN

You're kiddin me, man. Yeah? Where's his crib? Can I call him or
something?

BENNY

He's probably gonna be somewhere in town tonight. Oh look! (glancing in the direction of the bar) Jo's by the bar now. Check him out,
man

INT. BAR, PARADISE NIGHTCLUB, HARLEM - NIGHT

From Freeman's POINT OF VIEW, JO LAWSON is delightfully engaged in conversation with Jenny, whose charm oozes all over Jo, obviously moved by Jenny's grace, wit and style.

Freeman approaches the bar.

> JENNY
> (extends a gloved hand to the awestruck Freeman.)
> I don't believe we have met. I'm Jenny. (pauses and smiles knowingly).
> And this is my buddy Jo Lawson.

> JO
> Hey, Freeman, my man, I see you cookin' up there tonight. You look good.
> (he notices Freeman's eyes are fixed on Jenny.) You sound good too, man.

> JENNY
> I think I'm gonna leave you men to talk. (giggles an all but girlish titter).
> I need to go powder my nose! (laughs naughtily.)

Freeman listens as Jo babbles on about working with Eddie Vinson but his eyes follow Jenny as she makes her way through to the crowd.

INT. PARADISE NIGHTCLUB, HARLEM - NIGHT

Jenny makes her way to the table where her husband Milt Jackson is seated with others.

She looks intently at Milt, lights a cigarette, throws her head back and gives a half-laugh, looking in his eyes as he chatters.

She disappears within herself.

FADE

INT. BANDSTAND, THE ELECTRIC EEL NIGHTCLUB, SMALL TOWN, INDIANA - NIGHT

As the band nears the end of the KIDNEY STEW BLUES, Eddie "Cleanhead" Vinson thanks the audience and introduces his band, including newcomer Freeman Lee.

WE HEAR KIDNEY STEW BLUES (NO VOCALS)

INT. CAR [MOVING] - NIGHT

Freeman is sitting in the middle of the back seat, when a queasy feeling dawns on his face.

FREEMAN

Stop, man, I'm gonna be sick, man, I'm gonna be sick…stop the car, man.

EXT SMALL DESERTED ROAD, INDIANA - NIGHT

The car signals and stops on a lay by. Freeman rolls out and runs and retches.

INT. CAR [MOVING] A FEW MILES FURTHER DOWN THE DESERTED ROAD - NIGHT

FREEMAN

It's just me man, nothing bad, it's just this really long ride man, startin'
to make me dizzy.

EDDIE

Yeah, sittin' in the middle don't make it better. Crack a window, Jo.

JO

We're almost there. We're gonna sleep tonight, I'm beat too. Eddie, we
gotta do somethin' or tell your agent to do something about these long
jumps, man.

FREEMAN

Well, Jesus Christ! Look at that!

EXT. DESERTED ROAD, INDIANA - NIGHT

On the open countryside, a billboard sign with a cartoon of a "NEGRO" scampering away from a missile of vegetables, with the words: "NIGGER READ AND RUN! IF YOU CAN'T READ, RUN ANYWAY!"

FADE

EXT. THE GOLDEN HORSESHOE, SMALL TOWN, NORTH CAROLINA - NIGHT

The band members put their instruments in the car and depart.

INT. CAR [MOVING] HIGHWAY, NORTH CAROLINA - NIGHT

Freeman is seated in the front passenger seat, fatigue written all over his face.

FREEMAN

I'm tired, man, ain't no body wake me up for nothin' even if we get pulled
over by the cops, man, I'm too tired to drive. I'm gonna get me some sleep
before we hit New York.

He closes his eyes.

EXT. WESTBROOK'S APARTMENT BUILDING - DAY

As Freeman and Elmo ('Mo') Hope approach the building, a little boy runs towards them with a bugle in his hand.

> LITTLE BOY
>
> Look, I can blow too! (he demonstrates)

> FREEMAN
>
> That's really cool, that's good. But you've got to keep practising, okay?

> LITTLE BOY
>
> Okay, I will.

He scampers off to join the group of onlooking children, double-Dutch ropes suspended, games stopped, all eyes on Freeman and Mo.

INT. WESTBROOK'S APRTMENT - DAY

Mo and Freeman sip beers happily, Mo almost choking on his as he laughs. Westbrook enters through the front door.

> FREEMAN
>
> Hey, man, what's happenin' Westbrook. This is my buddy Mo, Mo this is Westbrook.

> MO
>
> Good to meet you, Westbrook.

> WESTBROOK
>
> Oh, pleasure to meet you, Mo. I don't know how to say this, man, Freeman, I've just gotta tell you. Freeman, I think Mo has been stealin' Smitty's clothes and pawnin' them for a fix - he's a junkie!

> MO
> (indignant)
>
> Me? Man, I'd never take another cat's clothes. Man, I didn't never pawn nobody's clothes. Ever! (jumping up, slamming the beer on the table.) You callin me a thief, man? I ain't gonna take this. See ya, Freeman.

Mo walks out and slams the door.

FREEMAN

What in the hell? What's eatin' you? You called my friend a thief? A thief? What the hell has gotten into you?

WESTBROOK

First off, Freeman, Mo is not your friend. He's a dopefiend. He's a dopefiend!

FREEMAN

Man, I make my own buddies, Westbrook I don't need you to tell me... what's gotten into you?

WESTBROOK

I'm tellin you Freeman, he's a thief. He's a dopefiend, a dopefiend! I know because he pawned two of Smitty's suits, because he was the only one who could do it, since you let him all over the crib like there's no tomorrow when you all doin' your dumb shit! I know he pawned' em' cause the guy at the pawnshop knows Smitty, and asked him when he was gonna bring the tickets. That little shitty-assed dopefiend

WESTBROOK (CONT'D)

told the guy at the pawn shop that <u>he</u> was pawning them for Smitty, cause Smitty got called to sick family in the South, all of a sudden like. Man, Smitty ain't got no family in the South!

FREEMAN

You're callin' my friend a liar and a thief? Man, I'm gonna have to split from here, man Westbrook, this time you've just gone too far, man! I know we goof off a lot in the day, but, man, we're workin' at night! I wanna come and go as I please, man. Let my friends in without any kinda goodie two shoes shit! I gotta find myself another room.

WESTBROOK

Freeman, Mo's not a friend of yours. You're just young and dumb and stupid and think you 're hip! Move on out if that's what you wanna do. One day we're gonna laugh about this the shit.

FREEMAN

I ain't gonna laugh no time, man, you called my friend a thief, you insulted him! He's my friend, man.

CLOSE TO:

EXT APARTMENT BUILDING, HARLEM - DAY

Freeman approaches the building, with his duffel bag in his shoulder. He rings the bell and waits. The door is opened by Milt Jackson.

> MILT
>
> Oh, yeah, what's happening, Freeman? The room's ready, the other guy left yesterday.

> FREEMAN
>
> Thanks man, you've really helped me out.

The door closes.

INT. HALLWAY, APARTMENT BUILING - DAY

Milt unlocks the door to a small, modestly furnished room, lacking all the warmth of Westbrook's. Freeman looks in, smiles and turns to Milt.

> MILT
>
> Yeah, it's a good room, a good price. The bathroom's down the hall. Keep your room locked. No telling who comes to see them folks upstairs. And the kitchen is at the end of the little hall there. (He points in opposite direction.)

> FREEMAN
>
> Thanks a lot Milt. You really helped me out. That Westbrook called my buddy Mo a thief. A thief!

> MILT
>
> But Mo is a thief! Jesus God, Freeman don't let him anywhere near here, y'hear. Mo's a dopefiend, man. He'll steal the milk out the coffee if you let him.

> FREEMAN
>
> You're puttin' me on, man, you've gotta be puttin' me on. Mo would take my things?

> MILT
>
> Mo will take anybody's things! The guy's gotta habit. You didn't know that? So, he steals to keep it. So, you comin' on down later?

> FREEMAN
> (disillusioned)
> Man, I guess so. I want to talk to Mo.

FADE

INT. HALLWWAY FREEMAN'S APARTMENT BUILDING - DAY

Jenny raps gently. With her ear to the door, she listens for life.

INT. FREEMAN'S CRIB - DAY

Freeman opens his eyes, looks around and closes them back again. Hearing a second rap, he opens his eyes and sits up.

> FREEMAN
> Who is it?

> JENNY
> It's Jenny.

> FREEMAN
> (leaping out of bed, into his pants and shirt)
> Oh, Jenny, hi. I'm just gonna be a second.

Freeman darts around the room, simultaneously zipping his fly, buttoning his shirt, splashing water on his face, rinsing his mouth and looking in the mirror to smooth his hair, he smiles.

INT. HALLWAY, FREEMAN'S APPARTMENT BUILDING - DAY

Freeman opens the door. Jenny and Freeman look into each other's eyes. Jenny breaks the silence with a soft laugh.

> JENNY
> Milt and some other cats are servin' up something to eat over at our place.
> They're fixing four for bridge later. Sonny says there ain't no way you
> two're gonna lose a game to me and Milt.

> FREEMAN
> Oh, yeah, sure. Milt says he's a big time cook. Yeah, I'll come on over.
> What time?

> JENNY
> Some of the other cats are there already. So, I guess whenever you're
> ready. I hope it's soon.

Jenny kisses her index finger and place it on Freeman's lips. He nibbles the finger and reaches out to pull her closer. He devours her lips.

FADE

INT. MILT AND JENNY'S PAD, SITTING ROOM - NIGHT

Milt, Jenny, Freeman and Sonny are seated in the middle of the bridge game. Others eat and watch the game.

> MILT
> Okay, let's see, hmm, I bid three of spades.

> JENNY
> Milt, that was a dumb, dumb play you just made. It doesn't make any tootin' sense to me.

> MILT
> Jenny, you don't know nothin' bout the game. I'm the one that taught you. Just play and quit fussin'.

> JENNY
> Quit fussin'? Might have been easier if I could make even the tiniest bit of sense of the game you're playin'. You're supposed to be playin' with me, Milt, with me. Not against me.

> MILT
> Shut up, Jenny! Cut it out! Are you playin' or not?

> JENNY
> No! I quit! (drops her hand all over the game).

> MILT
> Jenny, where're you going? C'mon, Jenny it's late.

Milt rises to put a contrite arm around Jenny who shrugs it off and slams the door as she walks out.

REACTION Sonny and Freeman - embarrassed at the lovers' tiff.

> FREEMAN
> Milt, take it easy man, I'll go after her. I'll go see where she went.

EXT. NEW YOR CITY STREET, BROOKLYN BRIDGE IN BACKGOUND - NIGHT

Freeman and Jenny stroll arm in arm like lovers.

WE HEAR LET'S BUILD A STAIRWAY TO THE STARS

They embrace and kiss passionately.

INT. FREEMAN'S PAD - NIGHT

Freeman and Jenny make love. The beginning of their coupling is innocent, tender sweet but builds up to a passionately frenzy, followed by sweet nibbles, tender squeezes and giggles.

INT. BAR, THE PARADISE NIGHTCLUB, HARLEM - NIGHT

WE HEAR STARDUST.

Jenny and Milt drink and chat with other patrons. Jenny glances around with a wistful smile, returns her gaze to Milt and blows out cigarette smoke with a long thoughtful breath. The entire group turns towards the bandstand.

INT. BANDSTAND, PARADISE NIGHTCLUB, HARLEM - NIGHT

WE HEAR STARTDUST and the trumpet section, Freeman, Art Farmer, Benny Bailey and Blue Mitchell approach the bridge.

BIG NICK (GEORGE NICHOLAS)
(shouting over music)
The tune is written D flat, let's hear it in E natural!

WE HEAR THE BRIDGE OF STARDUST IN E NATURAL

BIG NICK
Let's hear it in B flat! Got that, B flat!

WE HEAR THE BRIDGE OF STARDUST IN B FLAT

BIG NICK
Let's hear it in D flat!

WE HEAR THE BRIDGE OF STARDUST IN D FLAT

BIG NICK
Back to E natural!

WE HEAR THE BRIDGE OF STARDUST IN E NATURAL

ANGLE ON Blue Mitchell whose instrument is locked in his hand while he fiddles with the apparently stuck keys, outclassed by the key changes of the other trumpeters.

BIG NICK
Yeah, that's right, the tune was written in D flat, so to the top, D Flat!

WE HEAR THE BRIDGE OF STARDUST IN D FLAT.

Blue Mitchell's miraculously overcomes all issues with his stuck trumpet keys and joins in with the rest of the trumpeters as they return to the melody.

INT. PARADISE NIGHTCLUB, HARLEM - NIGHT

The audience, mostly black, move rhythmically to the groove, leaning forward in their seats. Most are pleased with what they hear.

INT. BANDSTAND, PARADISE NIGHTCLUB, HARLEM - NIGHT

Freeman leaves the bandstand midway through STARDUST and slips discreetly offstage.
EXT. PARADISE NIGHTCLUB, HARLEM - NIGHT

Freeman and Jenny stroll down a dimly lit street and kiss.

WE HEAR LATER FOR YOU

ANGLE ON embracing couple on a deserted street.

INT. BANDSTAND PARADISE NIGHTCLUB - NIGHT

A jam session with Milt on the vibraphone, Monk on piano, WILBUR WARE on bass, SPECKS WRIGHT on drums, Idrees Sulieman on trumpet, running through chords from LET'S BUILD A STAIRWAY TO THE STARS.

FADE

INT. FREEMAN'S PAD, NEW YORK CITY- NIGHT

Freeman and Jenny lie in a loose embrace in bed. The wind ruffles the curtain.

WE HEAR the silence of the night. Jenny kisses Freeman.

JENNY

Sweet, innocent babe. (crawling to lie on top of Freeman) You were such a sweet babe – till you met me. (titters) You didn't even want to take your trumpet (sits astride him in *double entendre*) out of its case before you met me.

FREEMAN

(chuckles)

Jenny, babe, I told you then, you're too hip for me, babe!

(He raises himself up to hug her and look into her eyes)

JENNY

You were, but you're sure not anymore - a cute dude from the boondocks! (laughs.) So, what's Ohio like, country bumpkin? I never went to Ohio.

FREEMAN

Oh, I don't know much 'bout it, seeing as though I only lived there for most of my life. (laughs)

JENNY

Okay, then, Wilberforce… what was that like…you had whitepeople there? I mean like real prejudiced whitepeople?

FREEMAN

No… Wilberforce was all black. I mean I come to New York and guys tell me, you know, don't show them white cats nothing, 'cause they're just going to steal it and make money! I didn't see any white people regularly in Wilberforce. No, I lie - there was one white guy there. He was married to a black lady - she didn't look very black, but she said she was so, I guess she was! (laughs)

JENNY

Oh, man, back in Indiana we had whitepeople. I mean real prejudiced whitepeople. They didn't live in my neighborhood though, we lived on the other side of the tracks. No black folks go to that other side too much, you know, unless it's to clean houses and shit. And, certainly no white folks come to our side! (laughs)

FREEMAN

Matter of fact, I never really saw real prejudice until I came to New York.

JENNY

(exasperated)

You've gotta be kidding, give me another one!

FREEMAN

Look, I grew up in a small town, it was a real little place, not more than 500 people, if you count the chickens and the hogs. (laughs.) Naw, but I mean growin' up in an all-black community, you know, who was to be prejudiced about what?

JENNY

You mean you never saw real prejudice until you came to New York a few years ago?

FREEMAN

Yeah, that's right. (pause) Naw, I lie. A white guy shot my dog.

JENNY

A white guy shot your dog?

FREEMAN

(sits up and lights a cigarette)

Yeah, my dog was Spot, man! Spot was my dog, man, he couldn't sit up and beg or nothin' he couldn't do any tricks but Spot was my dog, man. Spot was an outtasite little dog!

FREEMAN (CONT'D)

Anyway, I was like twelve years old, and I'm riding along on my bike and a white guy just came up and like - BOOM! (voice wavers) He shot my dog! And boy, I didn't know what to do. I never had nothin' like that happen to me before, and (laughs.) I was too little to beat him up. Besides, there were two of them!

REVERIE, TRAUMA MEMORY- 1939 - BLACK AND WHITE

EXT. OPEN COUNTRYSIDE NEAR WILBEFORCE, DIRT TRAIL - DAY

Twelve-year old Freeman pedals his bike, accelerating downhill. He takes his feet off the pedals and coasts. Spot, a nondescript dog of no discernible pedigree, races along behind the bike.

FREEMAN (silent)

C'mon, Spot, c'mon. You gotta keep up! I can't slow down now.

Freeman glances around to see Spot in hot pursuit.

He turns around to face forward and he sees TWO WHITE TEENAGERS approaching on his bike trail.

He removes his right foot from the pedal and comes to a halt.

White Teenager #1 raises his shotgun, aims at Spot and pulls the trigger. Freeman's face crumples in distress, he drops the bike and lets out a deafening silent bellow.

He runs over to Spot, hugs his lifeless body and looks up at the two youths now approaching, crying questioningly. He looks at White Teenager#1 who lowers the gun and laughs. White Teenager # 2 looks askance at White Teenager #1.

CLOSE TO

INT. FREEMAN'S PAD, NEW YORK CITY - NIGHT

FREEMAN'S gazes steadily ahead in silence.

> JENNY
> A white guy shot your dog just like that. Didn't nobody do anything?

> FREEMAN
> I don't know. I can't remember what happened. I went home to get my wagon and my eighth-grade teacher saw me and she said, "what's happening, Freeman" and I was crying, you know, and I told her that a white guy shot my dog.
>
> And she and everybody came over to my house and I don't remember, but something must have happened. I remember telling my Grandmother and my Grandmother was bad! I mean we lived right next to some Bishops, right, the President of the school lived right next to us! But my Grandma Mary didn't care nothing about those Bishops!

> JENNY
> You lived next door to Bishops - you didn't tell me you all were rich folks!

> FREEMAN
> Naw, we weren't rich. People thought we were rich, but we weren't rich. I mean my father was a bricklayer, my Uncle Freeman worked at the post office, my aunt was a school teacher, so we had money...

> JENNY
> What did Grandma Mary do? You told me 'bout everybody else.

> FREEMAN
> Grandma Mary? She just told everybody else what to do I suppose! (laughs)

REVERIE, GRANDMA MARY, 1939 - BLACK AND WHITE

EXT. FRONT YARD OF MODEST HOME, SPRINGFIELD, OHIO - DAY

An old truck is parked in the driveway, loaded with furniture. Two men lift a table onto the truck, under the direction of a diminutive woman with fierce energy.

EXT. BACK OF TRUCK - DAY

> UNCLE FREEMAN
> (raises a table)
> Up, up, up, easy, easy - raise it a little higher.

EXT. FRONT YARD OF MODEST HOME, SPRINGFIELD - DAY

A man below the back of the truck pushes the table, almost vertically, towards his counterpart on the truck.

> GRANDMA MARY
> (on tiptoes to get a better view)
> Be careful with that table. Don't get it scratched. Your father's sister left
> that table to me on her death bed. Raise it higher, HENRY, the legs are
> going to be scratched.

> HENRY (MR LEE)
> Yes, Ma, I'm trying. Big Freeman, raise it up a little.

As the table is lifted onto the back of the truck, Henry joins Uncle Freeman in the back of the truck.

> HENRY
> It'll be a warm day in January before she quits, Freeman.

> GRANDMA MARY
> (only head visible)
> You'd better tie it down with some rope, it'll slip along as we drive.

> BIG FREEMAN
> Yes, Ma. Henry, you heard our mama, get some rope.

EXT. FRONT YARD, MODEST HOME, SPRINGFIELD, OHIO - DAY

> GRANDMA MARY
> L'il Freeman L'il Freeman!

FREEMAN

Yes, Grandma Mary, I'm here.

Freeman raises a bone above the head of a black and white dog, Spot and Spot jumps at the bone but will not sit up and beg.

GRANDMA MARY

Where are the girls, Freeman? Girls, young ladies - where are you?

INT. BACK SEAT OF CAR - DAY

Two young girls are seated comfortably amidst mounds of boxes, heads buried in books on their laps. WE HEAR GRANDMA MARY'S VOICE, " JANE! MARY!"

JANE

We're here, Grandma Mary, we're ready to go.

EXT. FRONT GARDEN OF HOME, SPRINGFIELD, OHIO - DAY

GRANDMA MARY

Oh, there you are - right where you are supposed to be!

INT. CAR - DAY

MARY

(sotto voce)

Yes, Grandma Mary, we're right where we're supposed to be.

Mary looks at Jane and their mutual snigger evaporates with the approach of Grandma Mary, whose head appears at the front window of the car.

EXT. FRONT YARD. MODEST HOME, SPRINGFIELD, OHIO - DAY

Grandma Mary approaches the front door of the house, opens it, peers into an empty house, closes the door and locks it. She places the key under the mat.

GRANDMA MARY

L'il Freeman, you and Spot can ride with your father and uncle. I'll ride in the car with MR. SHAW who has been waiting so patiently. He'll need me to direct him.

FREEMAN

(excited)

Oh really? With Spot in the truck? Bye Grandma.

Freeman scampers towards the truck with Spot on his trail.

EXT. ATTRACTIVE HOME WITH A SIX - CAR GARAGE, WILBERFORCE, OHIO - DAY

The two vehicles pull into the circular unpaved driveway, horns tooting in unison, reflecting the general anticipation of the family.

Freeman jumps out of out of the truck as soon as it come to a halt.

> FREEMAN
> Wow! Look, Spot, a six-car garage!

INT. KITCHEN, LEE HOME, WILBERFORCE, OHIO - DAY

WE HEAR "I CAN'T GET STARTED"

Grandma Mary is seated at the dark wooden table, peeling vegetables which she slices into various shapes, tossing the peelings into a bucket. She scoops the vegetables together and slides them a simmering pot atop a charming antique stove.

WE HEAR A BLACK DISK JOCKEY ON A BLACK RADIO STATION commenting on the top trumpet tune.

> GRANDMA MARY
> (cooing)
> L'il Freeman! L'il Freeman!

She rises to switch off the radio.

> GRANDMA MARY
> (losing patience)
> L'il Freeman! L'il Freeman!

EXT. BACKYARD VEGETABLE PATCH, LEE HOME, WILBERFORCE, OHIO - DAY

Freeman, a watering can in one hand, pulls Spot by the collar away from a bed of sprouting lettuce. Freeman's tugging is awkward, as Spot has dug his heels in.

> FREEMAN
> Aw shucks, alright, Spot. Grandma Mary is calling. And when she calls
> like that, it means it's time to feed the hogs. C'mon Spot, let's go.

Spot relents and gets up as Freeman tugs him.

INT. KITCHEN - DAY

Grandma Mary leans out of the double-paned window and bellows Freeman's name and she turns around to see Freeman standing by the table.

> FREEMAN
> Yes, Grandma Mary, I'm here. I just had to get Spot to leave your vegetables, you know.

> GRANDMA MARY
> Well, Freeman, you know, if Spot 'plays' in the vegetables, those seedlings will be replaced, and those seeds will be paid from your paper route money.

> FREEMAN
> No, Grandma Mary, Spot tried to dig stuff up, but I prevented it!

> GRANDMA MARY
> (pinching his cheek)
> You prevented it! Prevention is better than cure as my mother always said.

Grandma Mary hands Freeman the bucket of hogslop which he reluctantly accepts.

> GRANDMA MARY
> The hogs have to be fed and everybody needs chores. Why, when I was your age…

> FREEMAN
> I know, Grandma Mary, you were making the stew and washing the floor and helping with Aunt Jane, and doing your lessons and…

FADE

EXT.VICINITY HOGS PEN, BACKYARD, LEE HOME – DAY

Freeman scoops peelings and generic hogslop into troughs.

WE HEAR APPRECIATIVE SNORTS OF HOGS.

Spot barks and wags his tail. As Freeman empties bucket on his second run of the troughs, Jane approaches pushing her bike which appears to resist.

FREEMAN

Oh, hi Jane. What brings you to this smelly hog pen?

JANE

Oh, Freeman, my bike's busted. The pedal won't move.

FREEMAN

So?

JANE

Okay, I was just thinking, you know, just wondering if you could fix it.

FREEMAN
(non-committal)

Maybe.

JANE
(restraining Spot's attempt to lick her face)

Freeman, don't be a mean big brother. I am just a girl and I can't fix bikes! Please!

FREEMAN

And if I fix your bike, you won't make me pay you a nickel to ride your bike, if I ever need to use yours for my paper route if my bike gets busted?

JANE

No.

FREEMAN

Promise?

JANE

I promise.

FREEMAN

Okay, I'll fix it but here - first you have to feed the hogs!

He hands her the bucket.

JANE

But, Freeman, I don't like hogs – they stink!

FREEMAN

You think I like feeding the hogs? Anyway, they're fed - you just have to wash the bucket.

JANE

You sure are one mean big brother.

WE HEAR MEAN TO ME.

EXT. A COUNTRY ROAD, WILBERFORCE, OHIO - DAY

Freeman pedals his bike with Spot trailing and skilfully throws a rolled newspaper onto a front porch. Spot barks in applause at the accuracy.

The next throw misses the target, Freeman drops his bike on the curb and runs to retrieve the paper stuck in a shrub.

EXT. FRONT PORCH OF CHEERFUL HOME, WILBERFORCE - DAY

As Freeman approaches the porch, the front door opens to reveal a petite light-skinned black lady, MRS. LEVY.

MRS. LEVY

Oh, my - what a surprise! Freeman, I'm so sorry I missed you the last few times. I have something for you, just wait right here. You're not in a hurry, are you?

FREEMAN

No, ma'am. I mean yes, ma'am. Oh, uh, uh, I can wait. (his eyes turn upward, and he snaps his fingers he recalls.) Oh, Mrs. Levy, ma'am my grandmother wanted me to ask MR. LEVY if he could take a look at the leak in the, uh, kitchen.

MRS. LEVY
(shouting and leaning backwards into the house)
BEN! Ben! Mrs. Lee needs your help.

Ben, a Jewish man, around 40, appears at the door and puts his arm on his wife's shoulder. He greets Freeman and Mrs. Levy goes inside.

BEN

Oh, hi Freeman. Tell Mrs. Lee I'll come by at seven o'clock to see about the leak. I've been meaning to drop by, but one thing led to another and…

Mrs. Levy returns to hand Freeman an envelope which he gratefully accepts and feels with both hands as if to calculate its contents, oblivious to Ben's words. He glances up as Spot barks.

FREEMAN
Yes, Mrs. Levy, I'll tell my grandmother that Mr. Levy will be over at, uh, uh…

BEN
Seven o'clock sharp.

FREEMAN
Yes, at seven o'clock. Oh, thank you very much, Mrs. Levy, thank you. Mr. Levy. I have to go now. I've gotta do the rest of my paper route now.

Freeman turns and runs, the pair chuckle and close the door.

EXT. COUNTY ROAD, WILBERFORCE - DAY

Freeman, pedals his bike at great speed, glances around to see Spot trailing. He skilfully throws the remainder of his cargo with accuracy, and [slow motion] drops his bike and runs and hugs Spot [end slow motion]

FREEMAN
We did it, Spot! We did it! Now I've got nine dollars and seventy-five cents saved up. Now I can almost buy my trumpet. Do you think Grandma Mary will give me a quarter if I do all my chores, feed the hogs, wash the bucket, water the vegetables, do my homework?

Spot barks.

FADE

EXT. SIDE OF HOUSE, CLOSE TO HEDGE, WILBERFORCE - DAY

Freeman puts a trumpet to his lips, raises it upwards and blows a few tentative notes of I CAN'T GET STARTED.

EXT. SECOND-FLOOR WINDOW OF HOUSE, WILBERFORCE - DAY

A 13- year old boy, PATRICK, appears at the window and blows a more polished rendition of the tune. He breaks and laughs.

EXT. SIDE OF THE HOUSE, WILBERFORCE - DAY

From Patrick's elevated point of view, Freeman replies, and his melody is smoother than his first tentative blow.

> FREEMAN
> Hey, Patrick, I just got it! C'mon over to my house and we'll play a duo.
> C'mon down!

EXT. FIRST FLOOR WINDOW, SIDE OF HOUSE, WILBERFORCE - DAY

From Freeman's *terra firma* point of view, Patrick laughs excitedly and pulls down the window frame.

INT. PARLOUR, LEE HOME, WILBERFORCE - DAY

Freeman and Patrick perform "I Can't Get Started", with Patrick leading as Freeman plays catch up.

Grandma Mary enters the room, unnoticed and at the end of the performance she does a solo applause, seated on the piano stool before a fine instrument which dominates the room.

CLOSE TO:

INT. STAIRCASE OF FREEMAN'S PAD, NEW YORK - DAY

Freeman and Jenny rub nose together tenderly.

WE HEAR MACK THE KNIFE.

They embrace on the landing of a winding staircase.

WE HEAR THE SLAM OF A HEAVY DOOR.

Freeman starts, Jenny withdraws from the embrace, puts her finger on her lips and points towards the door of Freeman's pad.

Freeman opens his eyes wide in disbelief and Jenny coolly goes into the apartment.

WE HEAR A MASCULINE ASCENT OF THE STAIRS.

Milt comes into view and goes up to the next floor.

> MILT
> Oh, shit, Freeman, what are you doing on the stairs sneaking around?
> You getting' high? Freeman, that shit is no good!

FREEMAN
(a bag of nerves)
Naw, man, I'm just getting ready to leave.

MILT
Freeman, don't try to kid me. I've seen guys just waste away on that shit. Cut it out, Freeman, that shit is just a bad scene, man, just messes up your insides.

Milt continues up the stairs.

INT. LIVING ROOM, MILT AND JENNY'S PAD - DAY

Milt is reading in an armchair listening to himself on vibraphone, when the door opens and Jenny glides into the living room.

MILT
Oh, it's nice to see you for a change.

JENNY
Oh, good afternoon, Milt. Nice to see you too, Milt. Please don't start.

MILT
Jenny, I'm worried about you. Where've you been? Getting high and shit?

JENNY
Milt, for God's sake, just let me! Let me be! I get high because I wanna get high. You don't get high because you don't want to get high. This is a free country I believe, or does that cease with matrimony?

MILT
Jenny, it's not about you getting high – it's just that…

JENNY
Cut it out, Milt. You fixin' for a fight or you want me to fix some lunch, so we can eat together like good ol' married folks.

MILT
I'm not fixing for a fight, Jenny, but I don't know where you are, what you're doing. If your family calls again, what am I supposed to say – sorry but I don't know where my wife is because we live like ships passing in the night?

JENNY

Don't make me laugh! Since when has my family been callin' <u>you</u> to find out where I am? Get off it, Milt! Playin' the sanctimonious husband don't cut no ice with me.

MILT

Jenny, I just got this feeling, I just know that you up to something, you're up to something... I just know'...

JENNY

Oh, yeah? Speaking of up, when was the last time you got up to something?

MILT

Damn it, Jenny. You got no respect for me. (slams paper on table.) I am gonna get out of here before I say things I'll regret.

He walks towards the door.

JENNY
(tearful)

Look, Milt, you better understand that I tried. I just wanted to sit down and eat without fighting...when you get back, this lunch will be cold. Lunch is not a vibraphone, you know, waiting for its master to take note!

Milt slams the door.

INT. FREEMAN'S PAD, NEW YORK - DAY

Freeman is asleep in bed. A few rays of sun illuminate the dark corners revealing beer cans, empty vodka bottles, one of which has a rose opening in full bloom.

The phone rings. Freeman answers.

FREEMAN

Oh, hi babe, it's you. I was just dreaming about you.

SCREEN SPLITS TO SHOW:

INT. BEDROOM, MILT AND JENNY'S PAD, NEW YORK - DAY

Jenny organizes clothes, mostly lingerie, with the phone in the crook of her shoulder. She is dressed and made up.

JENNY

Oh, babe, you know you're never very far away in mind and body. You know I'm always thinking of you, your sweet little trumpet.

FREEMAN

Oh (giggles) Jenny, you know it makes me go all goofy when you talk like that.

JENNY

So - you wanna go to Mexico?

FREEMAN

Mexico?! When - today? I can't Jenny, I am working tonight.

JENNY

How much you makin'? I'll pay you for the gig.

FREEMAN

But Mexico?! Jenny tonight, I…

JENNY

Live a little Freeman, babe! I'm packing right now. I'm gonna leave my bags at your place so Milt will be just as surprised as you are when he shows up and I'm gone.

FREEMAN

Okay, you got me. You got tickets and everything?

JENNY
(closing packed bag)
Of course, babe. I can't make you an empty offer can I? (giggles)

FADE

EXT. AERIAL VIEW OF ACAPULCO - DAY

An airplane descends

EXT. DESERTED BEACH, ACAPULCO - NIGHT

Freeman and Jenny stroll the beach arm in arm below a full moon.

WE HEAR LET'S BUILD A STAIRWAY TO THE STAIRS.

INT. HOTEL ROOM - NIGHT.

Freeman and Jenny make love in a tender, leisurely fashion.

The moon, all but full, is reflected in the gentle toss of the sea behind the silhouettes of Freeman and Jenny rubbing noses and giggling.

EXT. LA GUARDIA AIRPORT - DAY

A plane lands. WE HEAR WELCOME TO A LA GUARDIA AIRPORT.

INT. LA GUARDIA AIRPORT, VICINITY CUSTOMS - DAY

Freeman and Jenny, arm in arm and bags in tow, walk slowly, giggling and whispering while they wait, one passenger away from the CUSTOMS OFFICER. As the passenger is waved though, Freeman deposits their bags on counter.

> CUSTOMER OFFICER
> How long have you been out of the country?

Freeman starts to answer but Jenny beats him to it.

> JENNY
> I don't know…uh, let's see, we left on Friday, so I guess today is, uh, Monday, so I guess that's three nights and two days – Acapulco! Just great, no niggers except us two! (laughs)

> CUSTOMS OFFICER
> (he rummages through the bags)
> Who purchased your tickets ma'am?

> JENNY
> Not that it's any of your business, but I paid for them. Why, I just bought them with money.

> CUSTOM OFFICER
> (pauses and searches inside the bag)
> I see ma'am.

> JENNY
> Just be careful with your fingers. That bag has my best lingerie which I use to cover my private parts!

CUSTOMS OFFICER
(hands emerge from the bag with hypodermic needles)
And just what part of your private parts do you use these on? (turns to colleague) CHUCK, come over here…just take a look at these.

JENNY
Pardon me, but those are just needles. Just what they look like. No tricks.

CUSTOMS OFFICER
(grabbing Jenny by the shoulder.)
Come with me.

JENNY
(breaking free of his grip)
Excuse me, buddy, but is it a federal offence to have needles in a bag?

REACTION CUSTOMS OFFICER - Turning the bag upside down, he empties the contents and examines each item. Frustrated by the unfruitful search he turns away, as the colleagues indicates, by a swift hand gesture, that he is powerless to detain the passengers.

JENNY
Don't be an idiot! There's nothing else there! You're just gettin' off my panties, you pervert!

REACTION Freeman - embarrassed but amused

EXT. LA GUARDIA AIRPORT - DAY

Jenny and Freeman board a waiting cab.

INT. CAB [MOVING] - DAY

As the cab merges with traffic on the freeway, Jenny places a sign "JUST MARRIED" in the back window and Jenny and Freeman embrace for the ride.

WE HEAR NEW YORK, NEW YORK

INT. FREEMAN AND JENNY'S PAD, NEW YORK - DAY

Freeman and Jenny sleep entwined in a double bed, bathed by rays of sunlight squeezing through the gaps in the curtains.

There is a knock at the door. The couple turn over in deep sleep, still entwined.

Freeman pulls a pillow over his head with his free hand. The knocking persists. Jenny wakes up.

JENNY
Who is it? Good grief, its early - at least it's still early on this side of the
door. Could you go see who it is? I gotta go to the bathroom

Jenny unwinds from Freeman's arm and goes into the adjoining bathroom. Freeman groans and turns over, rolls out of bed, dons a robe and walks towards the door, the knocking persists.

FREEMAN
Who is it?

MALE VOICE
Listen buddy, I am sorry to bother you, but I just bumped into your car. It's
not bad, but I just thought, you know, you might need to get it fixed and…

Freeman opens the door and two WHITE MALES pounce on him, flashing law enforcement badges and restraining Freeman against the wall. Jenny emerges from the bathroom and screams and retreats.

FREEMAN
Hey, man, what's going on? What's happenin'?

LAWMAN #1
We have a warrant to search these premises for narcotics. We need you to
work with us. If you have nothing, then there's nothing to worry about
is there?

Freeman slumps against the wall and watches the two lawmen pull his tiny studio of a matrimonial home apart. Within seconds one of the lawmen finds a small bag with suspicious contents, examines it and shares his find with his colleague.

LAWMAN#2
(handcuff's out, grabs Freeman's arms from behind)
You are under arrest for possession of narcotics and I'm taking you downtown.

Freeman offers no resistance, looks across at Jenny who watches the scene aghast. He shrugs his shoulders.

INT. CELL, RIKERS ISLAND PRISON, NEW YORK - DAY

In a dark cell, Freeman lies on a single bed looking up at the ceiling. He recalls a funny incident and laughs.

He sits up and looks at the door, the small window of which is being opened to reveal the rather unimpressive face of a uniformed guard.

GUARD

Lee, it's time to eat. Five minutes, in the hall!

The guard unlocks the steel door and proceeds to the next cell.

Freeman rises from his bed, takes a leisurely comb to his hair, straightens his collar and leaves after his self-admiration is interrupted by "GET DOWN THERE, LEE! YOU HAVE TWO MINUTES OR YOU EAT SHIT IN YOUR CELL! STEP ON IT LEE!" growled by the Guard.

INT. DINING HALL, RIKERS ISLAND PRISON - DAY

WE HEAR THE DIN OF MEAL TIME.

The inmates are in a line, receiving servings of food from an array of assorted slop.

Freeman accepts his meal with resignation, looks up and recognizes JACKIE MCLEAN and ELVIN JONES.

FREEMAN
(approaching the duo)
Hey, man, Jackie, Elvin. Hey, you cats end in up this shithouse with the likes of me, man? Which block are you at? I am on E, man, E flat as a matter of fact, man!

ELVIN
(motioning trio towards chosen seating)
We are on B. Freeman, you got any salt, man, salt is real cool to have in this joint. Never knew that salt is the life of the earth till you come in this joint!

JACKIE
Yeah, Freeman, when'd you get here? You brought salt?

FREEMAN
Well no. I noticed they ain't put none in the food, so I didn't wanna ruin the unique flavor they've got there – is salt contraband or something?

ELVIN
I'm counting my days – first thing I'm go have me when I get out is real nice steak at Beefsteak Charley's. C'mon, Jackie, the screws aren't lookin' just let me have some salt, quick, pass it under the table. Thanks, man.

With a magician's flourish, he sprinkles salt over his and Freeman's meal.

FADE

INT. DINING HALL, RIKERS ISLAND PRISON - DAY

The trio rise and separate, they empty their leftover portions in huge buckets, stack their trays and join respective lines of inmates, who are frisked in sequence as they file out of the hall.

INT. MAIN HALLWAY, RIKERS ISLAND PRISON - DAY

Freeman files up the stairs to the third floor with guys from his block.

There is spontaneous jailhouse humor, as DRACULA, a stern-faced guard, hovers over an inmate whose conduct is arbitrarily deemed suspicious, but who is really acting up to the delight of the inmates.

Those on adjacent and opposing floors relish the spectacle of a slightly built inmate cowering, disingenuously, under the glare of the fiendish-faced guard. An entertaining event is made of the non-event of returning to isolation in the cells.

> DRACULA
> (embarrassed but all-powerful)
> Watkins, you're gonna be here longer than most - you still wanna fuck
> around? I'm gonna report this disruption to the chief — solitary in farm
> is what he'll recommend!

The inmates HISS and BOO.

> WATKINS
> Oh, beg your pardon, Massa, I couldn't walk. I just got me a pebble or
> something in my shoe.

He crouches, removes a tiny white pebble which he shows to Dracula.

The inmates' cheers fade into the rhythmic sequence of cell doors CLANGING shut on the lower floors.

FADE

EXT. RIKERS ISLAND PRISON - NIGHT

A convoy of cars pull up to main gate. A guard approaches the first, a chauffeur driven number, recognizes the occupants and offers a deferential wave as he signals for the gates to be opened.

The gates open and the convoy rolls in.

WE HEAR CARVIN' THE ROCK

INT. CELL, RIKERS ISLAND PRISON - NIGHT

In the dark, Freeman lies in bed, legs crossed, blowing trumpet exercises.
He takes a breath and becomes aware he is being watched by unseen eyes and is startled as he notices Dracula's' evil eyes looking through the square hole in his cell door.

> DRACULA
>
> Lee, you ready to go on down?

> FREEMAN
>
> As ready as I will ever be

Freeman rises, dons a shirt and goes towards the door which is now open.

The guard frisks him for contraband, looks around the cell and ushers Freeman out. The door closes to darken an already desolate prison cell.

INT. CORRIDOR INSIDE RIKERS ISLAND PRISON - NIGHT

From below, the view is of a brightly lit four-story rectangular corridor. The lonely figures of Freeman and Dracula pace slowly around the third-floor corridor to the nearest stairs, descend two floors and disappear behind a vault-like security door opened from the inside by another severe looking guard.

WE HEAR MISTERIOSO

INT. STAGE, AUDITORIUM, RIKERS ISLAND PRISON - NIGHT

The tattered red velvet curtain onstage shimmers to a SLOW DRUM ROLL and to WILD APPLAUSE and whistles from the audience, the curtain goes up to reveal a band comprising "jail house jazz musicians", including Freeman.

The band begins.

The lights spot a backdrop of a prisoner in prison stripes, seated in a stone quarry with a pick-axe, with the words THE SOUND OF RIKERS ISLAND in huge letters.

The inmate musicians play A NIGHT IN TUNISIA (Elmo, Freeman, Jackie, Elvin among them.)

INT. AUDITORIUM, RIKERS, ISLAND PRISON - NIGHT.

ANGLE ON the enthusiastic applause of the civilian audience of prison officials, whose spouses are the only female figures in the entire room.

FADE

SUPER:

1993
THE INTERVIEW

INT. LE BAISER SALE, RUE DES LOMBARDS, PARIS - NIGHT

Freeman and the Interviewer are seated at a table in stark white room. Prints of selected drawings depicting the slave trade adorn the walls.

WE HEAR AFRO BLUE

> FREEMAN
> We were in the penitentiary, miss, I keep telling you that. You're missing the whole point...

> INTERVIEWER
> You were there? You were busted?

> FREEMAN
> We were prisoners, convicts.

> THE INTERVIEWER
> You had your instruments?

> FREEMAN
> No, they had instruments over there. That's all I ever... one time I was in the bakery the first time, but after that I played in the band. That's all you did - you go down to the band room, just practice all day or play basketball, cards, chess, whatever.

> INTERVIEWER
> But it was a liberal regime inside?

> FREEMAN
> Shit no!! Liberal?! (laughs)

INTERVIEWER
How did you get time to do all this? Play basketball?

FREEMAN
I didn't have, I didn't have, that was my job!

You could have a job working in the kitchen, you could have a job working on what they call the seawall – oh there's plenty of things to do over there! And somebody got to run the place on top of that. Oh, they have got a job for you!

As I said, I was working in the bakery, which is a good gig, because it's right next to the butcher shop, and then you can go over there and get meat and stuff, and go over to the bakery and cook it, because the food in the mess hall!! I mean no salt! You don't get any sugar, you don't have salt and pepper on the table or anything like that. They don't put any in the food either! (laughs.) Some pretty rotten food but it ain't bad.

INTERVIEWER
It was a busting all together? How did you all end up there?

FREEMAN
That penitentiary - Riker's Island - the most time you can get up there is 3 years. If you get more than that you go up to Sing Sing or Attica – ever heard of Sing Sing? When you leave the police down there – what we used to call the Tomb – where the court house is, if you have over 3 years, you don't go to Riker's land, you go to Sing Sing or wherever else you're gonna go.

There's very few people, Sonny – that's Sonny Rollins – he got 3 years. He got more time than any guy I knew that was there. The rest of the guys got 6 months.

THE INTERVIEWER
Were you playing there on Riker's Island? In the band?

FREEMAN
Was I playing? I'm, I was playing in the band over there.

THE INTERVIEWER
(incredulous)
Riker's Island – the prison – had a band?

FREEMAN

Certainly! Why do you think they had all these guys... You're missing the whole point! Everybody has a job, right? In the kitchen, in the machine shop, bakery whatever. My job was the band!

INTERVIEWER

The band?

FREEMAN

That's it, the band was my job.

INTERVIEWER

Who else was there? How big was the band?

FREEMAN

Well, it depends, you know, uh, on who was in jail at the time! (laughs) I mean they have some guys who are just jailhouse musicians, they only play when they go to jail! (laughs.)

But you got Elvin Jones, Jackie Mclean and Hank Mobley -you got a bunch of cats over there that could play. Oh yeah. We used to have a good band...used to.

You ever heard of this place in Lexington, Kentucky where they used to send all the drug addicts? You've never heard of that? That was much cooler than Riker's Island because it was government for one thing. The food was outtasite! (laughs)

You go down and you get your eggs scrambled or turned over, you ain't get that shit on Riker's Island. You just got whatever they gave you!

Oh, I was down there for a couple months, (laughs) Lexington, Kentucky. Why was I there? I got busted, man.

I was at home in New York and these three white guys came by and they got a car from Philadelphia – the licenses plate – these guys got on turtle neck sweaters and shit, you know they got all…. Anyway, they say they want me to go cop and I say I ain't go cop.

So, I went. Uh, these guys were parked on Broadway and Seventy something street and I hop in the car and zoom!

FREEMAN(CONT'D)

A taxi cab pulled right up in front of us – police of course! See the gun in my face. I know I am cool, 'cause I know I ain't got nothing, right? I look down on the seat and there's these drugs sitting on the seat between me and this cat.

So, this could be anybody's, right? Of course, they took everybody. Everybody got arrested!

INTERVIEWER

You and the other guys?

FREEMAN

Yeah, but I'm the only black guy, y' know. The little tenor player says, "Man, I'll take it; I'll say it's mine and cut everybody loose!" That's great! So, we had to go down to court.

We get into the court room and this little guy's mother gets up - his mother sent a lawyer there and he got up to say something and the lawyer told him to shut up and took him out of there - he's gone! I don't know what happened to him.

So, that's three cats left. So, I say "Look, I am NOT going to jail, man, it's not mine." Two nights passed – boom! The other cat's gone. That leaves me and Danny. We're the only two with records. Those other cats ain't never been busted.

So, I knew it was his, he knew it was his. They had a program if you want to go to Lexington instead of going to Riker's Island and that's how I got to go to Lexington… Danny got to go to Riker's Island!

Danny was a piano player. The sax player's mother just came and took him away! He was the youngest, his mother just came and got him! The other sax player was the only guy there I knew real well. He was gone. That just left me and the piano player.

I knew I was going to jail because I had been there before, and (laughs), and they were going to send me right back! So, I went to Lexington instead.

INTERVIEWER

And Lexington had a better band?

FREEMAN

For one thing, I'm signing myself in, I can sign myself out! (laughs). I couldn't sign myself out of Riker's Island!

I didn't ever run into Billy Brooks the whole time I was in New York. I think I may have seen him once but that was because another guy from Cincinnati - I never knew Billy Brooks real well back then - till I ran into him in Amsterdam. Billy played with big bands. But Billy can do all that high shit, all that spectacular high note shit!

I can't do all that. I don't even know how to do it. But if you learn how to do it, let me know! (laughs).

THE INTERVIEWER
(trying to refocus from detour)
So, in Lexington, when did you have practice time?

FREEMAN

You mean in institutions? Oh, that's all you do is practice! Man, you don't just get up and get the band together and everybody plays.

I mean you just practise, and whoever is the conductor or the man in charge says play so and so and then you play, but most of the time you just practise. Man, because you can't play these tunes 8 hours a day! How well do you have to play theses tunes to practise them 8 hours a day, five days a week, man?!

I never played in the band in Lexington because I wasn't there that long. I just signed in and maybe only stayed a month or something like that. But, uh, Wilbur Ware wasn't in the band either. In fact, none of the three, none of the four of us were in the band. We played the show, but we didn't make any rehearsals. We just played the show.

THE INTERVIEWER
What show?

FREEMAN

I have no idea. It must have been Thanksgiving! I was only down there once. On Riker's Island they have a show for the inmates and then they have a show for the staff and their wives and stuff, assuming if the show was that good. Most shows were good because the gay people were really talented. Most of the gay people were talented, you know. They really put on a good show. It's not like the Apollo!

INTERVIEWER

But you said none of the four you at Lexington were in the band. All four of you played that show?

FREEMAN

Yeah, all four of us played for that show. Wilbur Ware played bass, Specks played drums and the other guy played guitar.

INTERVIEWER

Specks Wright?

FREEMAN

Yeah, he used to play drums with Dizzy. And Wilbur Ware. He made a lot of records with Monk. He's pretty well - known if you check him out. He was playing bass fiddle. Very good. Ah, you heard of Ron Carter? He hasn't got Ron's technique, but he swings more than Ron.

Oh, that Ron! He used to come to New York, you know, he didn't know anybody. The, uh, young lady I was staying with at the time, she knew him because they were both from upstate New York, Rochester. He used to come down to New York to cop and he told me one day, "Freeman, I wanna come to New York, I wanna… see if you can do anything, bla bla.. bla.." So, I got news that, you know, Chico Hamilton was in town and needed a bass fiddle player. So, we told Ron and he called Chico. Ron can really play. He never looked back after that.

But the cat hardly speaks now. Hey man…how are you doing "Yeah, Freeman." - gone!

INTERVIEWER

You don't see him?

FREEMAN

He doesn't have time to say … anything. (with sadness) It doesn't make much difference anyway. Now, where were we? (laughs)

FADE

EXT. RIKERS ISLAND PRISON, NEW YORK - DAY

The sunrise casts a golden light over the prison courtyard.

WE HEAR MUSIC.

A guard, armed and ready, makes an about turn to the sound of footsteps descending the metal staircase on the corner of the rectangular fortress which is Riker's Island Prison. The courtyard is deserted.

INT. CELL, RIKERS ISLAND PRISON, NEW YORK - DAY

Freeman is seated on his bed, smoking a cigarette. He looks around the bare room. He hears the rattling of keys, rises and walks to the door.

INT. BLACK CADILLAC, ENTRANCE, RIKERS ISLAND PRISON - DAY

Dressed in her finest, Jenny is seated in the back seat of the vintage automobile, consistent examination of her gloved hands her only sign of nerves, until she lights a cigarette from an elegant case and leans forward to the driver who obliges her with a light. She drags on the cigarette.

WE HEAR MUSIC.

EXT. ENTRANCE, RIKERS ISLAND PRISON - DAY

WE CONTINUE TO HEAR MUSIC.

A slow-opening, cumbersome grey metallic door is pulled back, revealing a stark courtyard and the lonely figure of Freeman, with a small bag, walking to freedom.

As he nears the threshold of the gates, he pauses, puts an exaggerated foot forwards, heel first and glides through to the outside.

The door of the car opens and Jenny runs around the back of the vehicle, all CLACKETY-CLACK in her heels.

Freeman breaks into a smile and they embrace, look into each other's eyes for verification of the moment and board the car.

Freeman, ever the gentleman, opens the door for Jenny.

INT. CADILLAC [MOVING], FREEWAY, NEW YORK - DAY

> FREEMAN
> Hey, man Wilbur, or should I say Mr. Hogan? I really appreciate your
> coming to get me in this, uh, very stylish automobile (laughs)

WILBUR

That's okay, man – it's the least I could do to get you back on your gig, man

FREEMAN

(squeezing Jenny's hand)

Well, I just hope I can get my gig back, as a completely and absolutely rehabilitated citizen of this great city of New York. (laughs) Don't tell me who got my gig, just tell if you know of any good gigs - I mean like Moody and shit?

WILBUR

Yeah Moody is working – he had this little cat playing trumpet, can't think of his name, you know the one that hangs out with Jo…

FREEMAN

With Jo what's-his-name. Yeah, I know the one…he got my gig? Well, I'll just have to see what I can do to get my groovy little gig back. (laughter)

INT. BANDSTAND, BIRDLAND, NEW YORK - NIGHT

JAMES MOODY and band including Freeman on trumpet are in the full swing of the gig with MUSIC.

INT. AUDIENCE, BIRDLAND, NEW YORK - NIGHT

Many well-known individuals are visible among the patrons such as Sidney Poitier, Ava Gardner, Frank Sinatra. Jenny is among patrons. They appreciate the musicians' efforts.

INT. LOBBY, JENNY AND FREEMAN'S APARTMENT, NEW YORK - NIGHT

Jenny closes the heavy door against the icy wind, removes her hat and shakes off a few snowflakes, removes a key from her purse and opens the mailbox.

She examines an envelope with care and ascends the stairs.

INT. FREEMAN AND JENNY'S APARTMENT, NEW YORK - NIGHT

WE HEAR MUSIC.

Jenny closes the door, removes her coat, pours herself a small one which she downs at once, shivers, sits in an armchair rubs her hands together and opens the envelope.

Her countenance changes to concern, she drops the letter on her lap and looks straight ahead. Resolved, she rises, puts on her coat and hat and departs.

INT. 'MUSICIANS' CORNER', AUDIENCE, PARADISE CLUB, NEW YORK - NIGHT

Monk, Idrees, Freeman and Mo and the others talk shop, during a jam session featuring Milt on vibraphone.

> MONK
>
> Freeman, you want a record date, man, or are you, uh, pressed for time these days?

> FREEMAN
> (laughs)
> Naw, man, I'm not doing anything these days I mean, I'm working, but I haven't got a record date since I did that gig with Mo. Who else is on the date?

> JOHN SIMMONS
> It's gonna be a real groove, man, I am on the date and Kahlil Amati, you know him, he plays drums with Big Nick sometimes.

> MONK
>
> Yeah, Freeman, we all know that John here was one of the first dudes to fiddle with Mr. Benny Goodman – so he's, uh, very (laughs) distinguished! From the rest of us that is! (laughter.) No, I'm kidding, just kidding John. I'm just puttin' you on. Uh, no offence intended! So, it's next Wednesday, what time do you all want to do it? We got two o'clock in the afternoon or we ten o'clock in the morning.

> FREEMAN
>
> Hey, man, the early bird catches the worm – ten o'clock man, where?

> MONK
>
> Studio on 54th. So now that that's settled, I am going to get my beauty sleep. (rises, bows and departs)

The jam session, which had wound down to a sax duo, suddenly picks after JOHN SIMMONS takes his bass fiddle and leaves company for the Bandstand. Everyone listens keenly.

Jenny drops in to join the men, she whispers into Freeman's ear and places a substance in the palm of his hand as they kiss, cheek to cheek.

> FREEMAN
>
> Indiana tonight? But it's late. You can't leave now, it's cold, it's late.

JENNY

I'll be okay, babe. She's sick, Freeman. Real bad. She took care of me after my mother died. She's like my mother. I have to go – tonight. It could be the last time I see her.

FREEMAN

(hugging Jenny)

Oh, Jenny, I wish I could come with you – do you want me to go with you?

JENNY

No, stay here and work. I don't know how long I'll be. A few days, maybe a couple of weeks. I have to go see her, be with her tonight. But I'll call, or even write if I stay away for too long. (laughs)

FREEMAN

Okay, I'll come with you to the station. Oh, Jenny, Jenny. (he kisses her cheek)

EXT. STREET, UPTOWN, NEW YORK - NIGHT

Freeman and Jenny walk arm in arm up the street, the neon lights on the Paradise Club visible in the background, in a light snowfall.

Jenny catches a few snowflakes in her hand, puts them to her mouth and giggles.

WE HEAR LET'S BUILD A STAIRWAY TO THE STAIRS.

They descend into the subway.

FADE

INT. BANDSTAND, PARADISE NIGHTCLUB, NEW YORK - NIGHT

Freeman and Mo join the band and experiment with the language of bop. The jam session is lively with a bass solo and a piano solo by Mo.

CUT TO:

INT. FREEMAN AND JENNY'S APARTMENT, NEW YORK - NIGHT

Freeman, in the half light of the dingy apartment is high with a number of nameless, faceless others. The men sit and lie in various poses, heads bowed, arms dangling in euphoria.

OVERHEAD ANGLE, Freeman collapses on the couch, numb to everything.

EXT. MAIN STATION, INDIANAPOLIS, INDIANA - NIGHT

Under the skyline of the city, darkened by smoke belching from chimneys, Jenny disembarks from a bus, a small bag in hand.

INT. MAIN STATION, INDIANOPOLIS, INDIANA - NIGHT

Jenny huddles against the cold and walks quickly to the waiting room.

She spots a few waiting cabs outside and uses the phone.

INT. FREEMAN and JENNY'S APARTMENT, NEW YORK - NIGHT

OVERHEAD ANGLE of Freeman, completely out of it, as he stirs to ringing of the unanswered phone.

INT. MAIN STATION INDIANAPOLIS, INDIANA - NIGHT

ANGLE ON Jenny's approach of and departure in a waiting cab, visible in silhouette with her trademark red scarf through the station's glass windows and doors.

EXT. STREET, INDIANAPOLIS, INDIANA - NIGHT

WE HEAR MUSIC.

A cab leaves for the deserted outskirts of the city where bare trees, dusted with snow, line the street.

The cab swerves onto the soft shoulder and does a U-turn.

INT. CAB [MOVING], STREET INDIANAPOLIS, INDIANA - NIGHT

Jenny smokes a cigarette and surveys the scene. There is anticipation in her eyes

> JENNY
> Next right, please. See that little neon sign up ahead? Hang a left there
> and stop.

> DRIVER
> You're sure, ma'am? This is a rough part of town.

> JENNY
> Yeah, I've got an old friend that lives here. How much'll that be?

EXT. A DARK STREET, INDIANAPOLIS, INDIANA - NIGHT

Jenny walks briskly along street, empty of all but a few drunks and a quantity of garbage. Snow falls gently.

WE HEAR RUBY MY DEAR.

She stops in front of a door, pushes and disappears inside.

INT. DARK LANDING OF STAIRCASE - NIGHT

Jenny emerges onto the landing from the stairs below.

WE HEAR THE SLIDE OF A BOTTLE ON A BLUES GUITAR.

Jenny rings a buzzer. A hostile figure opens the door and stands on the threshold.

>HOSTILE FIGURE
>Whaddya want, lady? Ain't no work in here for your kind. This is private property. Beat it!

>JENNY
>(unflappable)
>That's no way to talk to one of MITCH's friends. Mitch here? C'mon, let me in. I am a friend of Mitch from New York. (tries to push past the huge figure of the woman.)

>HOSTILE FIGURE
>Whaddya want with Mitch? He ain't here!

>JENNY
>Just tell him Jenny's here. He'll see me.

The woman closes the door and Jenny sways to the PLUCKING OF A GUITAR.

The door re-opens as Mitch, a rotund man of fifty, bejewelled to the gold tooth, revealed by a ghoulish smile, embraces Jenny and they go inside.

INT. CLANDESTINE AFTERHOURS CLUB, INDIANAPOLIS - NIGHT

On closer scrutiny, the 'club' doubles as the home of an unknown dweller.

Jenny and Mitch walk by a kitchen off the narrow hall to a large room, filled to capacity with men and women, draped in structured chaos on sofas, armchairs, folding chairs, crates and boxes.

A GUITARIST, with no other company than a bottle of liquor, teases eloquence from the strings of his guitar. Jenny greets an older female.

ANGLE ON the guitarist who SINGS THE BLUES, to intermittent YEAH, OH YEAH and CLAPS and FINGER SNAPS from the audience.

Jenny and Mitch depart, unnoticed.

EXT. DESERTED STREET, INDIANAPOLIS - NIGHT

A car pulls to the curb. Jenny alights, walks up the street.

EXT. A DARK ALLEY - NIGHT.

Jenny walks cautiously in the alley. She glances around nervously, and a cat runs across her path. She turns and runs.

EXT. DESERTED STREET, INDIANAPOLIS - NIGHT

As Jenny runs towards the car, her steps echoing in the silence against shabby condemned buildings, Mitch jumps out.

                    MITCH
    What's the matter? What's the matter?

                    JENNY
                  (breathless)
    Oh Jesus! Mitch, Mitch it's too dark down there! Mitch, I'm scared. I
    ain't going back. You sure them cats're really there? It's like a ghost zone.

                    MITCH
    You darn tootin' they're there. And they got good stuff. They're just
    hidin' from the cops. That's all. Now I'm waitin' for you – just be cool
    Jenny. I'd go myself but I owe'em money – they ain't want to see me!

                    JENNY
    Okay, Mitch, it's just that my aunt's sick, I gotta go to her place. Okay,
    just let me catch my breath. It's past the parking garage, big red door, two
    taps with the rock. (shivers) Okay, I'm ready. (kisses Mitch's cheek.) It's
    cold! But I'm go be warm!

                    MITCH
    Nothin' to be scared of – except alley cats. Its good stuff Jenny. It's worth it.

Jenny turns and runs breathlessly towards the alley.

EXT. DARK ALLEY - NIGHT

Jenny's pace is brisk, nervous. She approaches a graffiti covered metal door, stoops, picks up a rock and taps twice.

The door opens and three male figures jump out. One grabs Jenny's purse, the other two hold her against the wall.

ATTACKER #1
Scream bitch and I'll kill you with my bare hands.

Jenny shakes as if an ague, crying. ATTACKER #2 opens her purse and empties her contents on the ground. He rummages through her stuff like a wild animal. He finds money.

ATTACKER#2
Beat her up! That'll teach her to walk the streets! Fucking whore!

Attacker #1 and Attacker#1 deliver blows to Jenny. She falls to the floor, her back turned, her nails trying to grip the concrete walls. Attacker#2 kicks her in the back, her body crumples like a doll. She begs for mercy.

ATTACKER #3 holds her by her hair and bangs her head against the wall. Jenny falls face down, unconscious – she bleeds in the snow. The Attackers run down the alleyway.

FADE

INT. FREEMAN AND JENNY'S APARTMENT, NEW YORK - DAY

Freeman is asleep fully clothed atop the quilt.

INT. LANDING OF WESTBROOK'S APARTMENT BUILDING - NIGHT

Freeman, Jenny and Mo are on the landing.

Freeman raps at the door and blows his trumpet. Westbrook comes out of his apartment, angry at the disturbance.

Jenny does a dance, pirouettes clumsily, leans over the banister and falls into the darkness.

INT. FREEMAN AND JENNY'S APARTMENT, NEW YORK - DAY

Freeman wakes up startled. He shakes his head. He, looks at the clock – it is 11:45. He jumps up and shakes the fuzz from his head. As he panics through his morning ablutions he mumbles to himself.

FREEMAN
Oh God! It's tweeelve o'clock, I've got a date with Monk at ten. Oh, boy,
let them be late. Please, God, please let them be late!

EXT. ENTRANCE STUDIO, 54TH STREET, NEW YORK - DAY

Freeman runs towards a lone figure, fighting the shivers of winter.

                    FREEMAN
          Hey, Kahlil, what are you doing man, standing out here in the cold. We
          got a date with Monk!

                    KHALIL
          Freeman, the date was ten o'clock – it's after twelve now. Nobody can go
          in now. He's got Art on drums and somebody else, you know that dude
          that plays with Lester Young sometimes, on trumpet. We're too late,
          man, the date is over.

                    FREEMAN
          Aw, shit, man. I missed a date with Monk? What about John, did he
          make it?

                    KHALIL
          John made it alright. I saw him in there fiddlin' away.

                    FREEMAN
          John, man, the cat just lives a couple of blocks away from me, but that
          asshole didn't bother wake me up.

FADE TO

ENTRANCE, FREEMAN AND JENNY'S APARTMENT BUILDING - DAY

Freeman walks in an unsteady gait towards the door, he shivers in a light jacket against the light spring wind. His co-ordination falters and he struggles to open the door.

INT. LOBBY FREEMAN AND JENNY'S APARTMENT BUILDING - DAY

Freeman checks the mailbox, shuffles the contents and shakes his head. He ascends the stairs.

INT. BEDROOM, MODEST HOME OF JENNY'S AUNT, OUTSKIRTS OF INDIANAPOLIS - DAY

Jenny shivers under a blanket. Her face is swollen and completely disfigured by angry, swollen stitches all across her cheeks, forehead and chin. Her right arm is in a sling.

AUNT LOUISA approaches quietly.

                              AUNT LOUISA
                   (whispering and stroke her hair)
        Jenny, Jenny, oh, my baby. Look at what they've done to you. Oh, my
        baby! Oh my baby!

Jenny opens hers eyes and tries to smile but manages a grimace as pain overtakes the comfort of Aunt Louisa's presence.

                                JENNY
        Water. Water.

                              AUNT LOUISA
        Oh. Thank you, Jesus. Oh, thank you, Jesus. Yes, my baby, I'll get you
        some water.

She reaches for a cup on the table and cradling Jenny's head, gives her a few sips of water.

                                JENNY
        Oh, Aunt Louisa, the pain! The pain! It's too much. I need a shot from
        the doctor

                              AUNT LOUISA
        Here, take these. The doctor said they'll put you to sleep, Hush, baby,
        hush. Hush.

Jenny swallows the pills and slumps into oblivion.

INT. FREEMAN AND JENNY'S APARTMENT - DAY

Freeman enters, collapses into the armchair, his face with plump with water retained from an evening's high.

He goes to a night table, rummages through the drawer and among Jenny's personal belongings, he finds a notebook.

He looks at names, addresses and telephone numbers but does not find what he is looking for. He keeps looking through the notebook.

He puts down the notebook, looks at the telephone and then starts to practice on his trumpet. The telephone rings and he grabs it off the hook.

                              FREEMAN
        Hello, oh, what's happenin', Mo? You got what? Yeah, down by the park,
        yeah, it's a nice day out there today, man. Yeah, gimme ten minutes.

Freeman departs.

EXT. A PARK, NEW YORK CITY - DAY

Mo recognizes Freeman's familiar gait and rises. They exchange greetings and walk to a secluded section of the park. Mo pulls a joint from his jacket and lights up. The friends smoke a joint.

> FREEMAN
>
> Mo, you know, I'm really kinda worried, you know, I ain't heard nothing from Jenny - it's been over ten days.

> MO
>
> Freeman you just gettin' good and paranoid smokin' this shit. Jenny's just fine - where'd she go? Midwest somewhere?

> FREEMAN
>
> Yeah. Indiana - her aunt was real sick. But it's not like her, man, I'm not paranoid or nothing, but she calls her old man. (laughs) She's reliable.

> MO
>
> Funny, ain't it – Jenny is reliable and she gets high. Don't know 'bout you but some cats treat me like, you know, they kinda leery to hire me, because I get high sometimes. I mean, I never got so high I missed a date. Maybe a rehearsal, but not a date!

> FREEMAN
>
> Yeah, but Jenny's not a musician. But she's a fine old lady. (sentimental,) You know me, Mo, I'm a one woman man. You know you got cats that, you know, get a little bit here and a little bit there and…

> MO
>
> Freeman, you're getting all sentimental on me (sings in mock falsetto) 'All of Me, You to All of Me… (laughs before the third line)

> FREEMAN
>
> No, man, you got a lotta men that are one men women

> MO
> (laughing uproariously at the error)
> You mean like the gay cats? Naw, I'm just kidding but that was funny man, one men women

FREEMAN

Naw, I'm serious, man…you got high already off one little itty bitty joint, Mo?
(laughs.) I mean look at Monk man, that Nelly, she is like his right hand…

MO

I guess I never got no old lady to be my right hand (laughs) or my left,
because I stole from all'em! Man, I used to be real bad, man I wanna get
high I'd steal from….

FREEMAN

Mo, I know you stole, you stole Smitty's clothes when we had that pad on
Edgecombe. Or have you, has it slipped your mind? (laughs)

MO

I didn't steal them man, I just pawned them. (laughs) I was gonna get 'em
out. I was gonna get 'em out once I got money, man, really.

FREEMAN

(sneaks a drag from the roach and passes it to 'Mo)
This shit is strong, man, where did you get?

Mo drops the joint to prevent his fingers being burned and he jumps up as it lands in his lap. He comes face to face
with a uniformed policeman.

POLICEMAN

(bending over to hold the tiny roach between his keys)
Well, well, well. If it isn't Hope! What've you got here Hope?

MO

C'mon, man, you've gotta be kiddin'! As a matter of fact, that's a dead
roach, it ain't even mine, I never even saw it. Me and my buddy here we're
just enjoying the springtime and…

POLICEMAN

You'd better come downtown and uh, provide us with a statement. C'mon
now, boys, I don't wanna get rough, let's go.

FADE TO

INT. SQUADCAR [MOVING], NEW YORK STREET- DAY

Freeman and Mo sit handcuffed in the back seat.

MO

Look, gentlemen, twenty-five dollars, cash for the two of us. No, make that each, that's fifty bucks.

The policemen look around and laugh derisively.

MO

Okay, fifty bucks apiece... man, fifty bucks apiece that's one hundred.

The policemen look around and laugh.

POLICEMAN#1

Funny, how the traffic's flowin' real easy, as we're gettin' real close to the Tomb, huh? (sardonic laughter)

MO

Okay, man, seventy-five bucks apiece, man I got a record date comin' up, man, I'm gonna get some bread. Seventy- five bucks a piece and that's it man, my final offer. I ain't scared a no Tomb!

POLICEMAN#2

The Tomb is one thing, after that they're gonna dump your sorry little ass in Riker's and then the way I hear it, that will fuck up your cabaret card shit for a little while anyways!

Both policemen laugh.

FREEMAN
(elbowing Mo)

Gentlemen, let's just be reasonable here. I say, let's just say, we give you a hundred bucks apiece - we don't waste the city's time, the court's time, your time, our time…. (pauses for effect.) And then, when you actually think about it, if you book us, you'll be two hundred bucks worse off! And Mo's got a date this week like he said. I can, uh, raise my own, uh, dough.

The squad car halts. The two policemen alight, Freeman and Mo breathe a sigh of relief.

EXT. NEW YORK STREET - DAY

The policemen invite the twosome out of the car, undo the handcuffs.

Mo and Freeman quickly conceal their relief and look earnestly at two policemen.

POLICEMAN#1

Now, Hope, I know you, don't pull no shit! We want our money - two hundred bucks. On Friday! Any screw-ups and you've gotta take what's comin'...

MO
(a paragon of sincerity)
Naw, man, I'm gonna come up with the money...

FADE TO

INT. MO AND OTHER'S PAD, NEW YORK - DAY

A squalid L-shaped room, with a single bed, a table and three chairs, is the scene of a session of hedonism for four addicts.

The foursome, including Mo and Freeman have just shared a minute quantity of the drug.

ANGLE ON the battered door, where tissue paper fills the circular space left by an absent doorknob.

Suddenly, the tissue drops out of the door and Mo dives under the bed, though with limited success, as the weight of the trio atop make his manoeuvre clumsy and ineffective.

The policemen from the bust in the park burst in, and fortunately, the drug has been consumed and the paraphernalia has been hastily concealed.

POLICEMAN#1

Oh, let me see here now. We got one, two, three little niggers sittin' here. No bullshit, where is Hope?

FREEMAN

We don't know, man, we ain't seen him.

POLICEMAN#1
(viciously kicking Mo under the bed)
So, nobody's seen Hope! He's the invisible man! (kicks again.) Come on out of there, you little bastard, come on out from under this bed, or you gonna lie there and allow me to (he kicks) kick you silly...

Mo emerges undignified and humiliated from under the bed, holding his right shoulder. He is dragged away without resistance.

FREEMAN

Aw, shit, man these cops are like fulla shit! I raised my money... for some itty-bitty roach. Some of the guys put it together for me, but that Mo, man, he got money from a date but good old Mo. He ain't givin' up no money to them cops!

ADDICT#1

Man, it ain't too nice to think of what those cops gonna do to Mo, but, I don't know, man, this part's funny! He's hidin' under this itty-bitty bed, man - it's kinda funny, isn't it? His arm's sticking out here (demonstrates) his legs comin' out this end of the bed, he's pushin' up on me from under there. And those cops ain't getting' no money out of Mo!

The trio laughs.

FADE

INT. LOBBY, FREEMAN AND JENNY'S APARTMENT, NEW YORK - NIGHT

Freeman opens the mailbox, shuffles the mail and ascends the stairs.

WE HEAR LET'S BUILD A STAIRWAY TO THE STARS.

FADE

INT. SITTING-ROOM, AUNT LOUISA'S HOME, OUTSKIRTS INDIANAPOLIS - DAY

WE HEAR SWINGMATISM.

Jenny is seated in a rocking chair, staring out of the window. She moans and wails. As she turns her face we see signs of permanent disfigurement and gross scarring. Shivering, she pulls the blanket around herself.

AUNT LOUISA

Jenny, my sweet rose, you have got to eat. Here's some soup. Have a little. You need to get your strength back. The doctor's comin' later, don't want him to think I ain't lookin' after you.

JENNY
(shivering)
Not hungry. (moans.) Cold, Aunt Louisa, just cold!

AUNT LOUISA
(placing the back of her hand on Jenny's forehead)
But your fever's gone, honey. Why are you still shaking? You'll be feeling better soon. The doctor said that…

JENNY
(shivering, words garbled in sobs)
But I'm ugly, Aunt Louisa, I'm ugly. I look like a freak show! I can't even smile. (touches her face.) I'm ugly. From now on I'll be ugly. I need you to go and call Freeman in New York and tell him what an ugly wife he's got! (she weeps)

INT. FREEMAN AND JENNY'S APARTMENT, NEW YORK - DAY

Freeman, wistful, practices on his trumpet. He looks at the clock and rises and departs.

The phone rings unanswered.

INT. MUSICIANS' CORNER, PARADISE CLUB, NEW YORK - NIGHT

The boppers talk shop, gossip.

FREEMAN
But, no man. I'm telling you Bird is a genius, man, he can play, blow everybody away and he can talk about nuclear physics on top of that, man.

MO
Man, Bird gets high like, I don't know, like some of us and he talks a lot of shit like some of us…

IDREES
Naw, man, Freeman's right – Bird's a very talented, smart cat! He's very smart and I don't even know if he finished high school! Man, when he starts in that English accent shit, it makes me want to crack up but if you listen to what he's saying, then you'll see he…

MO
Idrees, man, how would you know if someone's really smart? You got a PhD or something?

FREEMAN
That's shit, Mo, and you know it. A man doesn't have to go to college to be smart and a man who goes to college doesn't have to be smart! Man, look at me (laughs) do you think I'm smart?

MO
(chuckles)
No, I think you are very dumb… you gave up money to them cops didn't you? Naw, I'm kidding, but I know what you're saying but most of the

time I can't even get what Bird is saying to me, and even if I listen he just goes on and on.

FREEMAN
That's because you're too dumb to catch Bird's drift!

The conversation fizzles and Sonny Rollins walks in and heads for the Bar. Freeman excuses himself from the table.

INT. BAR, PARADISE CLUB, NEW YORK - NIGHT

Sonny and Freeman greet each other and Sonny orders drinks.

FREEMAN
Hey, Sonny, what's happen'. Listen, man, I gotta thank you for putting up something for that little deal we cut with the cops last week. I really appreciate it.

SONNY
That's cool man, you know, I'm cookin' man, got two record dates last week got another one comin' up next week. I'm cookin', you know, doing it. You heard about Brownie?

FREEMAN
No, what happened to him?

SONNY
He died this morning in a car crash! Car just crashed, man, just crashed and Clifford Brown's dead!

Freeman is shocked, scared even. He shakes and folds his arms to steady himself.

SONNY
Yeah, Brownie is gone. Just like that BOOM! Freeman, oh god, man, Brownie was good trumpet player, could play his ass off. And he was a real nice cat. A really nice cat.

FREEMAN
Remember that time Sonny Stitt called him up onstage in that gig you had in Philly and he blew me away. Funny, and now he's just gone. A young cat too! Just blew me right off the bandstand! He's dead, man? It's kinda hard to believe.

SONNY

Bunch a cats're gonna go up to the funeral. His old lady's not doin' too well, evidently. I'm gonna drive. You wanna ride with us? Me and Jimmy?

FREEMAN

You know, Sonny, I'd like to go but I am kinda worried about Jenny. She went to Indianapolis to see her aunt but, man, I haven't heard anything, and I think I'm gonna go out there.

SONNY

She hasn't called? No letter? Just nothing? Man, maybe she found herself a new old man…(laughs) I'm just puttin' you on man. Man, if you're worried, man, you should check it out. Brownie's gone. Go check out Jenny.

FREEMAN

I'm gonna miss a few gigs, but I'm gonna split anyway.

SONNY

Freeman, I've never seen you like this, man. Drive safely, man, can't afford to lose any more trumpet players. If my old lady just split and I didn't hear from her, I'd freak out too. It's still snowy in those mid-west parts, she could be snowed in… anything.

FREEMAN

(finishing his drink]

I better go and get me some shut-eye. Man, I'm really sorry to hear about Brownie. Such a young cat. I got a long ride tomorrow. I don't want to be falling asleep at the wheel in redneck country. See you around, Sonny. And thanks again for help with that dough for the cops.

FADE TO

INT. CAR [MOVING] INTERSTATE HIGHWAY, NEW YORK STATE - DAY

Freeman drives listening to music on the radio.

EXT. INTERSTATE HIGHWAY, NEW YORK STATE - DAY

Freeman's car coasts along the highway.

WE HEAR MUSIC.

A sign indicates the border with the PENNSYLVANIA - DAY

Freeman hums I'VE GOT YOU UNDER MY SKIN and enjoys the scenery.

INT. CAR [MOVING] INTERSTATE HIGHWAY, INDIANA - DAY

Freeman smiles as he sees a sign ahead,

"WELCOME TO INDIANA". He scats a melody of his own creation.

EXT. A COUNTRY ROAD, RURAL INDIANA - DAY

Freeman's car negotiates a winding road away from the Indianapolis skyline, shrouding the sky.

The car stops near a small rustic house, where an old couple are seated on the porch. Freeman alights.

EXT. PORCH, HOUSE, RURAL INDIANA - DAY

The man gives Freeman directions with articulate gestures, smiles and tips his hat.

WE HEAR MUSIC.

EXT. DRIVEWAY, MODEST RURAL HOUSE, INDIANA - DAY

A modest house, isolated among fields of grass and trees deadened by winter. Freeman's car approaches, he toots the horn in anticipation.

EXT PORCH, RURAL HOUSE, INDIANA - DAY

Freeman looks around the porch and raps gently on the door.

He waits, turns his back to the door and takes a few paces to stretch his legs and arms. He yawns. He knocks the door again

WE HEAR THE RATTLING OF A BOLT.

The door opens to reveal a small child, shyly looking up at the stranger before him.

FREEMAN
Oh, hello little fellow, my name is Freeman Lee. Is your grandmother home?

The child nods slowly and smiling, he retreats into the house, leaving the door ajar. Aunt Louisa pulls the door wide open, her well-preserved face shows a striking resemblance to Jenny.

Freeman recognizes her resemblance to Jenny and extends his hand and introduces himself.

FREEMAN

Good evening, ma'am. I'm Freeman Lee, I'm Jenny's husband and, uh, a couple of weeks ago she said she was coming here to see you. (puzzled) I mean you are her aunt, aren't you?

AUNT LOUISA

(bursting into tears)

Oh, Lord have mercy, thank God you came, son I think you better come inside, son. Just come inside this house. Oh, Sweet Jesus!

Freeman follows the woman into the house and walks over to her and hugs her.

FREEMAN

Look, I am sorry ma'am, I didn't mean to intrude. I just drove here from New York to see Jenny…

AUNT LOUISA

Son, that's what I'm trying to tell you, you can't see Jenny no more…

FREEMAN

Ma'am, I know I didn't come and meet you and the rest of her folks before we got married, but we just sort of did it on the spur of the moment.

AUNT LOUISA

Listen son, Jenny is dead. She died, she just died, son (crying) she came in late at night and she was beaten up bad and robbed.

FREEMAN

Beaten up? And robbed? Where? Who beat her up?

AUNT LOUISA

(sobbing)

I really don't know. The police treated her like she was dirt, you know. She was in town, she came to see me, I wasn't feelin' too good… she was havin' a fit of the shakes – fever. (sobs) She died before the doctor came

REACTION FREEMAN - Freeman stares at the woman as if she were a total stranger, his disbelief and shock palpable. Tears well up in his eyes and roll down his cheeks.

FADE TO

INT. FREEMAN'S CAR [MOVING] HIGHWAY, INDIANA- DAY

Freeman drives, grief-stricken and shell-shocked, tears rolling down his cheeks.

He approaches a small, simple cemetery.

EXT. CEMETERY – DAY

ANGLE on a fresh grave, with wilted flowers.

Freeman attempts to alight from the car, but he fails, falls back into the car and weeps.

He continues to drive.

A sign YOU ARE NOW LEAVING THE STATE OF INDIANA is seen through his tears.

WE HEAR GOD BLESS THE CHILD.

FADE

WE HEAR BODY AND SOUL

As credits roll WE HEAR

                         FREEMAN'S VOICE
            Cats like Tommy Turrentine, Art Farmer, Fats Navarro, and Benny Bailey
            and Jo Gordon, they're blowin' cats away a mile a minute!

            You know, you didn't get up on the bandstand, I mean they kill and uh,
            the thing about it, you know, you play a song in B flat, they wasn't averse
            to changing it to B natural Or D flat or any key, which key? Find it and
            you just play it!

            You know, uh, let's play so and so and so - Body and Soul- you know you
            rarara and the bridge goes - somewhere off and you know, ah, you do that
            to some cat that don't know what the hell he is doing and…   Uh, you
            know Body and Soul is in D flat – play it is G Flat. Play it in A flat, play
            it in B Flat, anywhere A, E Natural. They are lost!

The End

Charles Freeman Lee

The Interview
Mid 1980s, with his sister
Professor Jane Lee Ball.

Freeman and Dutch guitarist, Wiebe Wilburs (*circa* 1992).

FREEMAN LEE
THE INTERVIEW

The following is the full text of an Interview of Freeman, taped at home in the 1980s in Yellow Springs, Ohio by his late sister, Jane Lee Ball Professor Emerita of English, Wilberforce University, Wilberforce, Ohio, United States of America.

The Interview is relaxed, intimate, and the free-flowing, probably because the Interviewer is his sister and not a jazz professional. He talks about the times, the clubs, the gigs, jazz and improvisation and his memories of the talents and personalities of others such as Monk, Bird, Elmo Hope and Bud Powell. He offers his own thoughts and experience of the art of jazz and bebop.

The Interview is preceded by an excerpt from *The Story of Jazz* by Marshall Stearns, including a quote from jazz legend, Louis Armstrong. The excerpt provides the context for the emergence of the revolution in jazz called bebop in the late 1940s through to the 1950s.

THE JAZZ REVOLUTION

This Revolution in Jazz - bebop - played itself out at Minton's Playhouse and the Paradise Club in Harlem, New York City from the late 1940s to the late 1950s. As contemporary jazz author Marshall Stearns said:

> *"By 1940, jazz had attained enough momentum and maturity to stage a revolution more or less within itself. No longer could the new developments be compared with reasonable accuracy to another wave from the South...For 'bop' was a sudden eruption within jazz, a quick but logical complication of melody, harmony and rhythm...The sounds of bop were literally unheard of and, accordingly controversial. The very word seemed to give offense... Musicians said the word was an imitation of a typical sound in the new idiom...Although the beginnings of bop can be traced back quite a way, the new style evolved with terrifying suddenness. Top notch jazzmen awoke to hear themselves sounding old fashioned, a horrid predicament in a music where you are judged by your improvisations. The advent of bop was not only sudden but also highly threatening to many established musicians.[2]*

Louis Armstrong, the great trumpet player, singer and composer referred to bebop as '*that modern malice*':".

> *"they want to carve everyone else up, because they are full of malice, all they want to do is show you up, and any old way will do as long as it's different from the way you played it before. So, you get all them weird chords which don't mean nothing, and first people get curious about it because it's new, but soon they get tired of it because it's really no good, and you got no melody to remember and no beat to dance to. So, they are poor again and nobody is working and that's what modern malice has done for you."[3]*

For a photograph of Freeman at the Paradise Club, visit www.ajazzmanstale.com. The photograph shows Freeman in the bebop scene at the Paradise Club, as he appeared in the October 1952 edition of Ebony Magazine.

---

2   *The Story of Jazz* (1956 Oxford University Press).

3   Downbeat, April 7, 1948, *Bop Will Kill Business Unless It Kills Itself First.*

Freeman at the piano with his trumpet at home in Yellow Springs, Ohio, United States of America.

(*circa* 1993)

The Interview with Charles Freeman Lee by Professor Jane Lee Ball

Professor Jane Lee Ball: The Paradise?

Charles Freeman Lee: The Paradise was a place where all the young musicians used to come.

PJLB: Such as?

Freeman: I went down there to the Paradise and Big Nick (George Nicholas) whipped that tune up, not If I Always, no – The Song is You – that is the one that went through all kinds of changes, that's the one I got pulled in on, I kept forgetting how the middle part went and how the first part went, you know. The first part wasn't too hard, the middle was really hard.

But, okay, Blue Mitchell came to town about a month after I did. All of us were brand new. Everybody except, I think…everybody knew…You never heard of Joe Gordon? Joe Gordon was up in Boston. Bad! Blue Mitchell from Florida – Bad! Tommy Turrentine - he's the one that blew down the whole Collegians, that time when went down there to Carnegie Hall. He sat in and blew the whole band away! Tommy is from Pittsburgh, his brother Stanley and Shirley played organ.

Clark Terry is supposed to be bad, he was playing with Count Basie or something. Clifford Brown? He hadn't come to New York yet, but no shit, when he came he blew everybody away! He's from Delaware. I got there, and everybody had heard of Joe Gordon and Tommy Turrentine and ah, they hadn't heard of Blue Mitchell, Clark Terry, all them cats from the St. Louis area, Miles Davis.

Anyway, I was up at my crib one day and this little dude came by - he used to like hanging around with musicians - and he said, "Hey, Freeman there is a bad dude down there he's blowing everybody away at the Paradise. Come on down!" And it was Blue. Blue Mitchell. Blue had one of those beautiful fat tones, like you know, a beautiful sound. Everything he played sounded beautiful! But cats that could really play, you know, like Howard McGhee – couldn't play shit – but we could play in all keys. If you wanna play Stardust in D Flat which is the original piece, you wanna play it in E Natural and its say the blues, it's all over.

We play the blues in a different key and it's all over for him…all you had to do with Blue was just change key.

I remember one time, Howard McGhee came 'round to my crib and said, "Hey man Roy Eldridge is playing so and so, so let's go and get him!"

All you had to do with Roy Eldridge was change keys on him and it was fun I suppose but…. (laughs).

When I got to New York, man, they were really obsessed by it, I mean Big Nick, when he called If I love Her, no not If I love her – Body and Soul, that's the one he got Bird with, but the Song is You.

I forget how it goes, but the bridge goes … tan tan - it starts out in Concert C and the bridge goes to D flat. To E to A flat to G flat you know – it's all those black keys on the piano so I'm playing all these funny keys on trumpet, I can handle that, you know. I am not bragging.

PJLB: I know.

Freeman: I am not bragging or anything, but Blue Mitchell couldn't handle it! Tommy Turrentine, Benny Bailey, I left him out. Benny Bailey – he could cook; Art Farmer, he could play. And we would all be up there playing when it came down to the middle, cats like you know Blue, Johnny Coles or that dude who used to pay with Lester Young, I can't remember his name.

Minton's Playhouse

I remember one time we were at the Playhouse, Minton's Playhouse, and me and Blue and Johnny Coles and Idrees (Sulieman) and Lou Donaldson. Lou could play in any key. And so. Elmo (Hope) was there. "Okay, let's do Cherokee." Cherokee is hard because the bridge goes …ta tan tan – that's all them black keys on the piano and you playing flats and sharps on the piano.

And funny thing is, Johnny Coles gets to the bridge and put his horn down and started patting on the keys and then when you get to the G chord, then his horn is workin' great!

He's patting on the keys to get through the D flat and E Flat and all those hard changes. When you got down to G and C7 back to B flat, his horn was workin' wonders boy!

Idrees? Idrees had four courses worked out. He's in the Jazz Encyclopaedia.

PJLB: Muslim?

Freeman: Yes. We were all young dudes in our early twenties and Idrees is running through all the courses. But me and Lou Donaldson and Elmo were sadistic - let's take these dudes as far as they could go!

Johnny Coles? He was cool, and he never did even try, every time he got to the bridge his keys would start sticking and he would just pat keys until he got down to the G and C7 and F7 chord and he was back in business again! (laughs)

And the dude that played with Lester Young - still can't remember his name - it will come to me, but it was four trumpet players, Lou and me and Elmo. I don't know who was playing bass fiddle and drums. But they were playing Cherokee for all those who could really play, you play as many courses as you want to.

Idrees would play four courses and quit because he had something fixed up for the bridge and you know the bridge was the only really hard part - the rest of the thing was nothing!

But the bridge was killin' folks, because they were playin' keys like D flat and G Flat and E Natural, you know you're playing keys that you're not really familiar with. I was cool in all of them!

I am not bragging. That's the reason I was really afraid when I first went there when George Russell was introducing me to cats, that were supposed to be, but he only introduced me to white cats but I didn't play… because…

Actually (Edward) Moon Mullens, when I started playing with Jack McDuff, you remember Candy Johnson and I started out and I ended up with McDuff. I told you about him pretending to shoot at that little dude in Louisville, right?

The Brown Derby, Louisville, Kentucky

Oh, it's a funny story, boy! We're down there, me, Moon and Glover and little dude - 17 years old Don Vendors from Cincinnati – could play his ass off! He died soon after at 21. Anyway… And we are all down there – Moon, I showed you that picture, he ain't had nothing that fit him he's raggedy, Glover's raggedy.

This little dude called Pork Chops I think, he was a dancer or some kind of entertainer and he comes in with this fine white broad and Moon up on the bandstand utters an obscene remark. (laughs.) This cat - a little dude really - he runs out of the club and comes back in with a gun but the Manager's stopped him at the door.

Okay, I'm young you know, 21, 22… anyway we are an after-hours joint called the Brown Derby and five us went down there – we were up there on the bandstand jamming, you know, stuff that we couldn't t do in the show. Don Vendors and me and Moon. I am young, I am dumb but, you see, I am loyal.

I am hanging out with Moon. These two little dudes come in with two other dudes. I forgot what he said to Moon, but Moon's got to see we 're outnumbered and I don't what he said but Moon jumped up and Moon said, "I'll talk about your mama".

Okay so Moon and I and these three others down there and I am easing Moon outta the joint – "Down that alley, man!' And we started down that alley and we hear these shots and those others down there in the alley shooting at us.

And luck just was with us, man, because down the other end of the alley, McDuff is getting out of a cab. Moon calls out "Hey McDuff, you got your gun?" and he said 'Yeah" and these others split. McDuff ain't got shit! (Laughs)

PJLB: Monk?

Freeman: Monk? Okay, Monk introduced himself to me. It's funny, isn't it? I was pretty good. Everybody intro-Leonard Feather introduced himself to me, Ira Gitler introduced himself to me. Bird came up and said "Hi. I am Charley Parker" and I said I was Freeman Lee and he knew me.

Monk had a record date and me and John Simmons supposed to be on it and the cat that played drums with Big Nick – Kahlil Amati – and John Simmons on bass, me trumpet and Monk said you wanna make this record date 10 o'clock in the morning or two.

The Paradise

We're all in the Paradise, and I say 'yeah, man 10 o'clock. Okay, now, I am really young, and I am not used to any of these things that are going on and the Paradise doesn't close till four.

And so everybody came over to my house and drank and stuff and when I finally wake up, it's tweeelve o'clock and I go busting down there! And they got that dude that played trumpet with Lester Young, I can't think of his name – I'll think of it shortly. Kahlil didn't make it. Art Blakey made it, he played drums.

Johns Simmons made it, naturally. John is, if you really go back to those… he was one of the first black dudes to play with Benny Goodman. He was a bass fiddle player with Benny Goodman. Yeah, John and he made the record date! But that asshole didn't bother to wake <u>me</u> up! (Laughs) I blew that one!

I blew another record date with Monk because I was on the road with somebody else and I don't know who – maybe Eddie Vinson or James Moody – and anyway I came back to town and Monk said he wanted me, Blue Mitchell, Sonny Rollins and Charlie Rouse to make this date.

And you have heard how Monk's music sounds, right? Can you imagine how it looks on paper? So, I say to Monk, "I can't play that." And he says, "Blue Mitchell can play it." I said there is no use for me to even try, to even attempt it. The record date, I don't know if he made the record, I don't know the tune, but it went something like tan tananan doin doin and trumpet players cannot do that shit! Sax players could, but trumpet players could not make – toin da dun – they just couldn't make those kinds of jumps - it's impossible!

So, when Monk tells me Blue Mitchell can play this music I'm like, wow! So, I run into Blue and I say, "Blue, you could play that stuff, that music Monk gave you?" And Blue says, "No, man I can't play that, but Monk said <u>you</u> could play it." And I said, No, man, I told Monk I couldn't play it either. So, Monk ended up doing a trio or something with him and the others.

Have a Drink at the Bar?

I played a couple of gigs with Lou Donaldson. Sax player, little like Bird but really not - a really good sax player. Lou Donaldson is one of the few cats like Horace Silver – didn't drink, didn't smoke so he would get gigs and I think Universal was booking him. And so, we had a gig over in New Jersey. Benny Harris was on the gig, Monk was on the gig and Lou.

At any rate, we got off the gig and maybe it was intermission and me and Monk and Benny went to this bar – this all-white bar - and they didn't want to serve no blacks at the bar and this was New Jersey!

I mean if you went to New Jersey, they're going to think you're an escaped convict or something!

Anyway, they asked me for ID to prove my age, to prove I was over 21 and I must have been about 23 or 24 at the time! Monk got indignant and of course Benny Harris got indignant, and I don't remember how it all got resolved - what happened, whether they served us or not. I don't really remember how it was resolved…

This was either intermission or after the gig one of the two, and we went to the bar to have a couple of drinks and they were not going to serve no blacks at the bar! Monk was 30 something so he said, 'Serve me!".

Monk, Mo Hope and Bud Powell

Monk is sort of macho in a dumb sort of way, if you ever met Monk, I don't know how he is now, he and Charlie Parker were two very strange – I don't want to say strange…

But Monk would do stuff like he would go out and play some basketball out there with the kids… he was very like Wilbur (Ware - very unorthodox doing anything, but he was effective! He could make baskets and you wonder how the hell in the world did he do that?

But he was… Horace Silver and all the cats – Horace Silver – all the dudes come by his house and you know I mean, there is some fine white woman, we would all get bombed. Monk didn't get bombed, he had his little rum and he had his piano and he would sit down and play stuff.

And he would show me, he'd start showing me stuff, you know, he would just sit down, he was very patient, you know. "What is that music?" and he'd just take it …and he'd spread his fingers – you would wonder how in the hell he did that shit!

One of the most memorable times I had with Monk, Elmo had just gotten out of jail - and he wasn't strung out or nothing - he was fresh from practising and he and Monk got to it, boy, and Elmo, boy, he really cooked! I mean he was cooking, Elmo was…

PJLB: You mean he was better technically than Monk?

Freeman: Yeah, he was better technically than Monk, man. I mean he was just – his fingers were just flying over those keys! And another time me and Monk and Bud Powell and some other cats. Anyway, I don't know how it happened but we all went up to Bud's pad, and Bud had this baby grand and we were all playing.

I copped out immediately. I figured I was good but, man, you know, Monk said play and I knew he could cook better than me.

Then Bud sat down, and Bud just wiped everybody out COMPLETELY! I mean bzzz bzzz, just, just I don't know - it's like you meeting Shakespeare!

I mean it's really is something, cats that can really. Monk was cool, but Bud - when Bud sat down and played, it was all over!

PJLB: Was he better than Art Tatum?

Freeman: Was he better than Art Tatum? Oh, well, you see I never heard Art Tatum play in person. I've heard very technical piano players play in person like Phineas Newborn Jr. He was very technical, I mean very technical, but Monk and Bud and those cats – Bud was technical, but he gave the appearance of being sloppy. You know, if you listen to Bud playing, he sounds like he may be missing notes or this that and the other whereas Phineas Newborn and Art Tatum were very exact with whatever they were doing. You know, which to my way of thinking, sort of detracts.

PJLB: Perfection detracts?

Freeman: I played with Sonny Stitt. Sax player. Sonny Stitt is perfection. Sonny Stitt rarely makes any bloopers at all. Frank Foster rarely makes any bloopers, but I don't think Frank Foster's reasons for not making bloopers is the same as Sonny Stitt's. Sonny Stitt plays the same thing over and over and over.

If you take a classical pianist - they play things over and over, they play the same thing over and over and over again. You ain't supposed to make bloopers! Art Tatum, I get the impression that everything he has played, he has played before. Sonny Stitt. anything he plays I know he has played before, because I played with him. And I know he practises the same thing over and over and he plays them without any mistakes – he doesn't goof off on them at all!

Charley Parker

Ah, Charley Parker, I never heard anybody blow a horn like Bird. If you heard Charley Parker play, you would fall in love!

Just from his - he stands there with that saxophone and he doesn't even look like his fingers are moving and he is just going all over that thing, but, man, his fingers are just barely moving - and he would be ripping through notes! And I mean anything! Bird could do anything!

I watched this program on television with Dizzy Gillespie and he was talking about how he was always interested in chords and he said when Charley Parker came to town everything just fell into place and that was it for Charley Parker.

You know, on that show everybody mentioned Charley Parker, but nobody mentioned Monk, you know, - actually without them two dudes, there wouldn't have been any Dizzy Gillespie! There wouldn't have been any Bud Powell, I don't know, maybe Bud, because – ah do you have those records I made with Elmo? Well Elmo and Bud grew up together and they are both very similar in their playing. They don't play anything like Monk.

PJLB: Nobody does!

Freeman: Yes, they do! That dude that died, I can't remember his name - he made a couple of records - I can't remember his name. He took somebody's place in Sonny Stitt's band when I was in the band. When I first got into Sonny Stitt's band, it was Horace Silver, Wilbert Hogan, Sonny Stitt and Connie King - I think that was his name, a bass fiddle player – he was the worst! (laughs) Couldn't play shit but he had a car! (laughs)

PJLB: That's funny!

Freeman: No that's the truth! Sonny Stitt had a good band except for the bass fiddle player, he couldn't play shit.

PJLB: But he had transportation – that's terrible!

Freeman: No, it's the truth! Anyway, this bass fiddle player had record dates with Coleman Hawkins for instance. I can't think of his name, King I think, Connie King. I don't why but I know he became a policeman in New York. Anyway, he couldn't play a goddamn thing on bass.

I was in so many bands with sad-assed bass fiddle players. Eddie Vinson's band – uh the piano player – Jo Lawson - he couldn't play shit. Charlie Rouse? Ever heard of him? He made all these records with Monk. Anyway, Rouse is in there and he didn't know shit and Rouse had been around Billy Eckstine's band, he was with

Dizzy Gillespie. He was a good reader, he didn't know how to - he was like Blue Mitchell. He could play the blues but if you play anything with changes in it, forget it because you know, he wouldn't know where in the hell to go – D flat, that sort of thing.

Anyway, Rouse was in that band with Eddie Vinson, me, Rouse, Jo Lawson, Hogan and some cat named Carl on bass fiddle - he couldn't play shit with me and Hogan. Hogan was a drummer. He and I were tight. Hogan could play his ass off. Hogan was with Lionel Hampton's band, he was with Ray Charles too.

Anyway, one time, I remember, I was so sick man, waiting for Jenny to come home with some dope and she phoned and told me, oh no, she's been busted.

PJLB: I know that feeling!

Freeman: Anyway, I am sick, man, had no dope. You get real sick when you don't have it. I ain't got no money. I am laying up there sick and shit and Hogan was working in one of the pit bands in them shows on Broadway. I got on the phone and his old lady answered and said he wasn't home, but she would give him the message.

Sure enough, he got home, and he called. I said, "Hogan, I am sick and broke, man". And he said, "Okay, Freeman, I'll be around." And I was staying on 49th Street and he was on 45th Street two or three blocks away and he came 'round, laid some bread on me so I could go out and cop. That's how tight we were.

PJLB: What about singers?

Freeman: Singers? I ran into a lot of them.

PJLB: You didn't work at Birdland, did you?

Freeman: Sure I did! Jazz Encyclopaedia said I worked at Birdland!

PJLB: Excuse me, excuse me!

Freeman: Yeah, I worked Birdland. Singers, I worked with Dinah Washington, Ruth Brown, Eddie Vinson. The one I disliked was Ruth Brown.

PJLB: Why?

Freeman: Well, this is the time we went to Chicago in them Cadillacs I told you about that broke down all the way? Okay.

So, I am staying with Johns Simmons, who is my buddy, so we miss rehearsal. Yeah, I don't know if you ever heard of Jesse Belvin and Bobby Freeman? These cats sang rock 'n roll and were in the show too. Now, all these people had their own accompanist. Ruth Brown didn't plus her music was not written out in chords - which is the shit I can read - but it was written out in regular piano music which is notes. I cannot see bass clef and treble clef at the same time.

PJLB: Were you her piano player?

Freeman: Yes. Plus, the light went out on the piano and so consequently, I messed up her music something terrible! (laughs.) And she felt very angry and she wanted me fired in fact, but I was cool with everybody else and actually the only thing I had to play was the band number and it was a tap dancing number and I played that. F 7, G7 or whatever they want to call, wasn't any big deal, I just ran through the notes!

But hers, Ruth Brown's, was like I had to read each note up and down you, know, three, four, five six notes in one time you know, they're just coming. You know - now, I hadn't rehearsed it - I don't know how this shit goes! I didn't have to worry with Jesse Belvin or Bobby Freeman. I was cool with their music.

But Ruth Brown, she thought I stank! Which I did - I have to admit! I really blew her music, most of the time, I just sat there looking at it - what in the hell is this? Probably by the end of the week, I was probably playing most of it, you know, we were only playing three shows a day so I had plenty of time to look at it! (laughs)

PJLB: What about run ins with law enforcement?

Freeman: I tell you, man, I used to work with a cat who used to play Broadway and he had a Cadillac and they used to bust us going back to New York. Every week-end they stopped that Cadillac because they were a bunch of black men in there in a Cadillac! That's why when they stopped us, I got indignant about the whole thing - because I wasn't going to open that trunk!

No, naw, take me to jail! You know, because they didn't have any reason to pull us over, no reason for it - they just did that to black men in New Jersey!

PJLB: Did you ever run into Charlie Mingus – he was supposed to have been quite the character?

Freeman: Mingus? I didn't know Mingus. I don't think I ever met Mingus. I know that, ah, at some stage there I remember, Miles went sort of berserk and he punched Paul Chambers, a bass fiddle player - excellent! – in the nose and blacked up both eyes and he went to some place and jumped Max Roach.

And Max was drunk, and he beat up Max. But Max got sober and went down to Miles's crib and was trying to kick the door in. Now, uh, Miles wouldn't pull anything like that with Mingus! Mingus, from what I heard about Mingus, Mingus didn't have any sense whatsoever you know, he would beat you up if he had to!

I was in Chicago once with Moody's band and Mingus was playing up the street and Jackie McLean was with Mingus and I went down to hear him. But I never met Mingus. When I did see him, he was a big kinda fat dude.

PJLB: Did you tell me that Sarah Vaughn and Dinah Washington didn't like each other very much?

Freeman: Sarah Vaughn? No no no, that is something that I read that Lena Horne said. Now you see, Billie Holiday - she is a dopefiend and all that stuff, right so -, you ain't never been a dopefiend so you really don't know how certain people really ostracize you! Like I couldn't get a lot of jobs in New York, why? Because "he's a dopefiend, he's not resp…he's not dependable." I guess Billie Holiday needed all the friends she could get. Sara Vaughn was not going to be the one to stick her neck out, according to Lena Horne. I played with Billie once in some dive joint, she did Blue Moon and all that shit. But Billie lost her union card and for a really long time she couldn't sing anywhere! Years, no kidding! I mean, you talkin' 'bout a jazz singer – if she can't sing for you, what's she gonna do? To them jazz ladies, their singing is like breathin' – you can't sing without your union card, so what's Billie to do?

PJLB: What about Sammy Davis Jr - ever run into him?

Freeman: No I never met Sammy Davis. Never met him.

PJLB: No? I thought you told me he was a nice little guy.

Freeman: Oh, I know all the guys say he was a nice guy. Like Billy Eckstine, you never heard anybody say anything bad about Billy Eckstine, you know.

PJLB: You just went to New York City – how would you describe New York from your perspective then as opposed to when you first went there?

Freeman: As compared to now? I don't know. Since I saw Dexter, Dexter Gordon, play and that's the way he's always played. All the other guys are playing whatever they think Coltrane was supposed to be playing or whatever they thought Sonny Rollins was playing. I don't know what the hell they're playing - something surrealistic I guess! But Dexter is very down to earth.

PJLB: You're talking about the music scene, I am asking about New York. The atmosphere now as opposed to when you went there in your 20s?

Freeman: Well, you see, when I went there in my 20s, everything was very new. And you know, there was the gridiron building and Lindy's and 52nd Street – Birdland! You don't have any of these things now - Beefsteak Charley's and all that. Last time I went to New York I ran into Sonny Greer in a bar.

PJLB: The drummer from Duke Ellington's band?

Freeman: Yeah, him - he's like a wizened old dude but lively!

PJLB: He is still playing, isn't he?

Freeman: Probably, I don't know. He came to the bar and I was hanging out with Howard McGhee and he ordered us drinks and stuff. McGhee introduced me to him.

And McGhee got sick – cancer I think – but his old lady, you know, you can't drink, smoke, you know. I just don't see that makes a lot of sense – they're gonna die anyway so why not just let them go out happy? Bombed?

PJLB: Why not go out bombed? Good note to end this part!

Wilberforce University

*The Oldest Historically Black University in the United States founded in 1856,
seven years before the Emancipation Proclamation, issued
by President Abraham Lincoln*

Alma Mater of
Charles Freeman Lee
Class of 1949

Home of Wilberforce Collegians

Vintage Photographs - 1890 - 1965

These photographs are courtesy of a licence from the National Afro-American
Museum and Cultural Centre, Wilberforce, Ohio, United States of America.
This museum has one of the largest collections of African-American materials,
including the largest African-American doll collection and over 9, 000 artefacts,
art and 350 manuscripts. The collection includes the typewriter Alex Haley
used to write *Roots*, a Buffalo hide worn by a Buffalo Soldier
and Gregory Hines's tap dancing shoes.
Visit www.ohiohistory.org

Wilberforce University Campus *circa* 1940 - a view of the main administrative building.

Wilberforce University was established in 1856, seven years before the Emancipation Proclamation. The town of Wilberforce, Ohio was an important community for African-Americans, as it is reputed to have had seven stations on the Underground Railway. The Underground Railway was a clandestine network of people and safe houses, offering shelter to African-Americans heading to Canada, to escape slavery.

Bishop Daniel Payne, President of Wilberforce University from 1863 to 1877, *circa* 1888.

The African Methodist Episcopalian Church was a founder of Wilberforce University and appointed Bishop Daniel Alexander Payne as its first President. He had been part of the courageous and visionary decision of the African Methodist Episcopalian Church to purchase the institution in 1863 outright, and "run it ourselves". He was the first African-American President of a college or university in the entire U.S.

Wilberforce University, Mathematics class in progress *circa* 1893.

Slavery had been abolished some thirty years before this photograph was taken and the number of females in the mathematics class is surprising, even by twenty-first century standards. Slavery had been abolished a mere 37 years prior to this photograph and many of these students' parents would have been slaves.

Wilberforce University Faculty *circa* 1890.

The Faculty included 6 women, a rare feat in the late nineteenth century, when very few women had the opportunity to attend or teach in a university.

Wilberforce University Faculty *circa* 1910.

Wilberforce gave the opportunity to these academically gifted men and women - who were rarely, if ever, given academic positions in traditional institutions - the ability to publish their academic writing and educate African Americans in the sciences, for the professions and for leadership.

The interior of the Carnegie Library at Wilberforce University, *circa* 1920.

This photograph shows the collection of newspapers in the library reading room, at a time when all was segregated by race - including journalism. One can imagine that many newspapers were from the African-American press such as *The Pittsburgh Courier, The Baltimore Afro-American,* and *The New Amsterdam New York News.*

Bishop John Andrew Gregg, President of Wilberforce University from 1920 -1924, *circa* 1920, second from left in front row.

This photograph was taken at Tuskegee Institute, Alabama, U.S.A. under the sculpture of Booker T. Washington - *Lifting the Veil of Ignorance*. Bishop Gregg served as a second lieutenant in the Spanish-American war, and wrote *Of Men and Of Arms*, a chronicle of his visits with wounded soldiers on various fronts during World War II. The visits were made at the invitation of President Franklin Roosevelt.

Wilberforce University Orchestra *circa* 1890.

This image of a pre-jazz orchestra at Wilberforce University confirms that musical ensembles in African-American universities pre-dated jazz and that music was a central part of academic life on campus. The Orchestra would have played ragtime by African American composers like Scott Joplin and later, James Reece Europe, described by renowned ragtime composer Eubie Blake as the "Martin Luther King of Music", for his leadership in organizing African-American musicians at the turn of the twentieth century.

The Wilberforce University Orchestra *circa* 1905, at rehearsal.

The presence of so many females in the Orchestra at such an early date in music history is remarkable. The music of James Reece Europe, Eubie Blake, Scott Joplin and others may well have reached these musicians, as their music had been published by Kentucky men, Ernest Hogan and Ben Harney, in 1895 and 1896. Jazz, on the other hand, often travelled by word of mouth as fans listened to live performances.

The Wilberforce Singers performing at a local Ohio radio station in 1939.

World War II was in progress but the United States had not yet entered the war. The Wilberforce Singers were less popular than Wilberforce Collegians, but they toured extensively to raise funds for the University. A notable member, Bayard Rustin - a civil rights leader and co-organizer of the 1963 March on Washington - was described as "one of the undoubtedly greatest tenors the race boasts" by an African-American newspaper in Jacksonville, Florida after a performance by the Wilberforce Singers.

Wilberforce University student body *circa* 1945 in front of Bundy Hall.

Bundy Hall was constructed in 1917 and was designed by noted Ohio architect Frank Packard. The building housed administrative offices and classrooms. In 1862, Wilberforce University had closed its doors as many students had enlisted in the Union army. It re-opened in 1863, after it was purchased by the African Methodist Episcopal Church under the leadership of Bishop Daniel Payne and James Shorter.

Students sitting examinations in the Gymnasium of Wilberforce University *circa* 1945.

Some male students are dressed in military uniform and were part of the Reserve Officers' Training Corps (ROTC) program at Wilberforce University. Wilberforce was one of the first African-American universities to have a Reserve Officers' Training Corps.

Bishop Ormonde Walker, President of Wilberforce University from 1936-1941, second from left, *circa* 1940.

He is photographed with military men in charge of Wilberforce University's Reserve Officers' Training Corps, the first to be established in an African-American University just prior to World War II.

This is a photograph of one of the first black fraternities in the United States, Beta Kappa Sigma in 1908.

The "Black Cats" as they were known, was never officially recognized by Wilberforce University but was forerunner for later fraternities. Lieutenant Charles Young, the third African-American West Point graduate, is second left in the second row. He rose to the rank of Colonel and taught military science at Wilberforce University. Controversy surrounds his non-deployment during World War I and many believed that white officers' refusal to serve under his command was a factor in his non-deployment.

The Carnegie Library on the Wilberforce University campus, *circa* 1940.

The Carnegie Library is listed in the United States Register of Historic Places. The building was a gift to Wilberforce University from philanthropist, Andrew Carnegie. It was constructed in 1907 and extended in 1938. The building still exists and houses the administrative offices of the National Afro-American Museum and Cultural Center, the very source of these historical photographs of Wilberforce University.

A Student in the Payne Chapel *circa* 1965, named after Bishop Daniel Payne, the first President of Wilberforce University.

A stained-glass image of a stylized, African Moses with the Ten Commandments dominates the entire chapel. Attendance at chapel was not a requirement for students.

Shorter Women's Dormitory *circa* 1930, the site of Freeman's first heartbreak.

Goaded by his fellow basketball practice mates, who told him another guy was visiting his girlfriend during basketball practice - the same time as Visiting Hours for the Women's Dormitory - Freeman skipped basketball practice to find out for himself. She was indeed seeing someone else and Freeman walked away, taking refuge in the school band, Wilberforce Collegians, which included jazzman Frank Foster.

Professor Yvonne Walker-Taylor, center, *circa* 1965 with students in the Carnegie Library.

Professor Walker-Taylor delivered the eulogy at Freeman's funeral in 1997. She was the first African-American woman to be appointed President of any university in the United States. She served as President of Wilberforce University from 1984 -1988. Professor Walker-Taylor graduated at 19 from Wilberforce University and after several advanced degrees, she joined the academic staff at Wilberforce in the 1950s. She was a gift jazz singer who compared her voice to Ella Fitzgerald's, but she ultimately chose an academic life. Her father, Bishop Ormonde Walker had been the 10th President of the University, making them the first father-daughter university Presidents anywhere in the United States.

Bishop Ormonde Walker, father of Professor Yvonne Walker-Taylor and Tenth President of Wilberforce University, second from left in the back row, *circa* 1940. He served as President of the University from 1936-1941.

EPILOGUE

Now that you have reached the end of this book, I hope that you enjoyed Freeman's story and now see how much fun jazz can be.

If you developed a bit of a *jazzitude* [4] after reading this work, so much the better. Life is complex and the ability to improvise is just another string for your bow.

Maybe the next time you hear a jazz tune, inspiration will descend. It may ask you to take that tune into your heart and really listen, as the jazzmen and jazzwomen meander around the melody, twist it, twirl it, duck from it, run from it and even turn it inside out and upside down. They improvise in the moment, creating with all the skill that practise has made perfect.

If it works for music, how about your heart? See if it is telling you that it may be time to leave that worn out melody that keeps playing in your life – maybe you can start improvising for a change. Why do it the way it was done before? Why do it the way everybody else does? Can you improvise in your life?

If that next jazz tune really moves you, spread the word. Jazz is cool! Jazz is accessible! Jazz is life!

Let's Make Jazz Fun Again! ™

---

4 A *jazzitude* is the ability to live one's own truth, improvising on one's formal learning from school, media, pals and parents. It is a combination of jazz and attitude, coined by the writer to give a name to jazz's relevance to life - when in doubt about the tune laid out before you, improvise!

BIBLIOGRAPHY

Equality by Statute—Legal Controls Over Group Discrimination, by Morroe Berger, 1953 Wash. U. L. Q. 117. This article was published 2 years before Brown v Board of Education and sets out the issues which the US Supreme Court failed to grasp in Plessy v Ferguson, the 1896 case which upheld segregation until 58 years later in Brown v Board of Education. Brown was argued on December 9, 1952 and the unanimous decision was delivered by Chief Justice Warren on May 17, 1954. Berger was way ahead of his time as a notable sociologist, Arab specialist and jazz scholar who toured the Middle East with the multi-talented jazzman, Benny Carter, on a State Department sponsored tour in 1975.

The Rise and Reform of the NYC Cabaret Cards in The Creative Life of Law: Improvisation, Between Tradition and Suspicion in Critical Studies in Improvisation Vol 6 No. 1, by Dr. Sara Ramshaw, (PhD University of London). **See** www.criticalimprov.com (Portuguese, Spanish and French)

The Rise and Reform of NYC Cabaret Cards is also published as the second chapter of *Justice of Improvisation* (Sara Ramshaw, 2013 Routledge)

The Story of Jazz, Marshall Stearns (Oxford University 1956, a Mentor Book)

Glorious to View: Wilberforce from 1856 to the Twenty-First Century, Professor Jane Lee Ball (Escudilla Publishing, 2010)

The New Edition of Encyclopedia of Jazz, Leonard Feather (Bonanza, New York 1959)

The Encyclopedia Yearbook of Jazz, Leonard Feather (Arthur Baker, London 1957)

All photographs of life at Wilberforce University – faculty, students, the Orchestra – were licensed from the National Afro-American Museum and Cultural Center in Wilberforce, Ohio, United States of America. These photographs are no longer available for licensing and their publication is unique to this book.

Made in the USA
Columbia, SC
06 December 2018